From Religion
Back to Faith

From Religion Back to Faith

A Journey of the Heart

BARBARA FIAND

A Crossroad Book
The Crossroad Publishing Company
New York

The Crossroad Publishing Company
16 Penn Plaza – 481 Eighth Avenue, Suite 1550
New York, NY 10001

Portions of chapter 2 will also appear in a forthcoming volume from
Twenty-Third Publications, edited by Stephen Honeygosky.

Printed in the United States of America

The text of this book is set in 11/16 Galliard.

Library of Congress Cataloging-in-Publication Data

Fiand, Barbara.
    From religion back to faith : a journey of the heart / Barbara Fiand.
      p.   cm.
    Includes bibliographical references.
    ISBN-13: 978-0-8245-2417-3 (alk. paper)
    ISBN-10: 0-8245-2417-9 (alk. paper)
    1. Spirituality. 2. Spirituality – Catholic Church. 3. Christian life.
I. Title.
    BV4501.3.F52 2006
    248.4′82 – dc22

                            2006024394

1 2 3 4 5 6 7 8 9 10   12 11 10 09 08 07 06

In Loving Memory of
Dorothy Stang, SND de N
Martyr

Contents

Preface

The future enters into us
in order to transform itself in us
long before it happens.

— Rainer Maria Rilke

It is a strange fact of my experience that my deciding to write a book is always the very last step in its formation. Instead of planning to write on a particular theme and then setting out to do research for it, I seem, almost synchronistically, to engage a topic for years on end — or perhaps the topic engages me — with never a clue that anything will ever demand writing. In many respects, books seem to gestate within me. They appear in lectures, retreats, and sometimes even as variations or minor themes of previous books, where they quietly prepare themselves for expression. My "journey of the heart" and its longing to move "from religion back to faith" was no exception to this experience.

The title of the book was not evident to me for a long time until, at last, the journey of *my* heart brought it to light. I have no intention, of course, to abandon one for the other, that is, religion for faith. I simply sense a desperate need in Christianity generally, and Catholicism especially, to retrieve faith, to see it for what it was always meant

11

to be, to bring it back from exile, if you will, and have it restore us to life and to the full maturity of believers who will then, and only then, be able to allow religion to assume its rightful place as well.

This book is not an easy read. I prepared for it — without realizing it — for about fifteen years. In *Embraced by Compassion* (1993) I wrote of our hunger for a retrieval of wonder, of our need to celebrate the mystery that is life itself and to accept the responsibility and compassion that accompanies its embrace. I discussed the dualism of our tradition that created a theology divided against itself and in need of heart. *Prayer and the Quest for Healing* (1999) attempted to touch this heart. It was intended for *courageous* hearts especially — those willing to step beyond the "same old, same old," to reflect deeply concerning the faith issues of our time. We probed into the paradigm shift offered us by the new sciences of the twentieth century and tried to see what insight they could offer us regarding the power of prayer, especially healing prayer. *In the Stillness You Will Know* (2002) expanded this topic, addressing specifically "the interface of religion and science," encouraging us "to understand deeply, through our very bloodstream, as it were, our interconnectedness with all of creation, with the universe, in fact, and come to grips with our mutual responsibility."

The present book leans on its "sister books" and continues, as well as expands, the questing begun in them. It is clear that both religion and faith are primarily human phenomena, and I wish to honor them as such. Nevertheless, although some of the topics discussed certainly embrace other religious traditions, the scope of this book will not permit a detailed discussion of all. Its general focus is, therefore, more restricted. This, I must confess, is primarily due to my need to stress the areas where my own Christian/ Catholic context presents the greatest concern for me and, therefore, allows me to write most meaningfully.

Chapter 1 focuses on the "dangerous memories" that center our faith in the Christ event. We wonder what actual effects they have on our lives and on the world we live in. "Is the world a better place because we believe?" is the central question of this chapter. "And if it is not, why not?" is the question that challenges us to take seriously our power for transformation.

Chapter 2 places us in our time and in the circumstances affecting our present global reality. It explores the meaning of faith as a primordial event of human consciousness, sees its connection to spirituality, and distinguishes it from religion with which it is often too quickly identified. We attempt to see the relationship between all three religious phenomena, how they are different, why they need each other, and what their place might be in today's world.

Chapter 3 is intended to provide us with the "Grand Option" for authentic community offered by the Christ vision of our early beginnings and reiterated by the evolutionary perspective of Teilhard de Chardin. It compares this vision with the reality of church as it is experienced today. This chapter was, by no means, an easy one to write and, I suspect, will not be an easy one to read. It will, hopefully, lead to honest discussion and an equally honest desire for both structural and personal transformation.

Chapter 4 speaks to the need for expanding horizons and identifies the extraordinary difficulty experienced in responding to today's mandate to "see with new eyes." This is true for everyone, even for those willing and eager to give themselves over to the transformation required. The importance of symbol and metaphor for religious language is discussed in this context and is compared to the objectivist/literalist approach of the past several centuries. By way of example, we reflect on the ascension of Jesus into heaven and Mary's assumption and try to see these within the context of today's emerging worldview.

Chapters 5 and 6 are, as I see it, the primary chapters of this book. Chapter 5 attempts to present, as simply as possible, the perspective offered to us by science today, exposing us to a worldview very different from the world perspective within which Christianity first articulated and "finalized" its beliefs. Because of the difficulty in changing what one has been taught to see, I offer in this chapter a series of true stories that hopefully can assist in opening up a new way of perceiving. The chapter is entitled "An Invitation to Wonder," and that is precisely what it is about, since wonder is the beginning of and necessary prerequisite for the humility that enables transformation.

Chapter 6 invites us, finally, to walk into the Christ Story and make it our own. We concentrate on our response to the question, *Who do you say I am?* And we realize that it takes courage to face the unknown and to surrender to the mystery. We try to accept honestly what we cannot know about Jesus and here have to deal with the misconception that anyone actually "owns" a final copy of the truth.

We distinguish between Jesus of Nazareth and Jesus the Christ, and we try to move beyond objectivism, literalism, and dogmatism, toward celebrating a different and perhaps somewhat unfamiliar way of empowerment and validation of the Christian Story. We stress our need for involvement with the "original impulse" that inspired the ministry of Jesus and explore the meaning of being about "the reign of God." In the process of these reflections we invite a reconsideration of the meaning of Christian table fellow-ship, of incarnation and the celebration of Christmas, of redemption and redemptive suffering, that is, atonement.

As I mentioned already, new ways of seeing are not eas-ily achieved. One primary difficulty for religious writings on this topic is that they cannot easily depend on the peren-nial support of former interpretations — the tradition — as proof of their own validity. The major difficulty for us today is precisely that the ground of, and rationale for, ancient interpretations is literally slipping from under us, and much of "what we have always understood" simply no longer holds. This book is a humble attempt to make the transition to new ways of seeing a bit less frightening and a bit more hope-filled. The "consolation" in what often can appear as "desolation" is that, in a world where everything is changing, our God may, in fact, be a "transformative" God in the very center of the movement, a God who is with us on the journey and whose love will not abandon us, whose Word continues to be spoken to bring light for the life and well-being of all.

Participation and dialogue are indispensable tools for transformation. Each chapter in this book, therefore, ends by identifying certain issues that I feel are in particular need of the reader's response and can serve well for discussion groups, sharing, or even quiet reflection. Quite often these identified issues consist of direct citations from the chapter and can, therefore, also serve as a review of the main points addressed there.

As always there are many to whom I am much indebted. I am particularly grateful to those friends of mine who helped focus my thinking with probing questions and helpful ideas, among them especially Joanne Schuster, Kay Brogle, Maureen Sauer, Joan Marie Sasse, and Karen Vaske. Thanks also to those who endured my lack of availability with patience and love. Writing is an arduous task that demands much discipline and concentration. Thank you for letting it happen. As a strong believer in the communion of saints I want to thank also those of my loved ones who have passed on but are still with me in the quest for global transformation. Among them most especially and always I remember Clare Gebhardt and her sister, Jeanette Nelson, Wilhelm and Elisabeth Fiand, Leon Lajoie, Pierre Teilhard de Chardin, Ron Terrence Colloty, Lois Weber, Clara Brunelle, Clara Heidelman, and now also Dorothy Stang, the martyr of Brazil to whom this book is dedicated. As always I am grateful to Crossroad Publishing Company for its support and encouragement.

❦ O N E ❦

Introduction

On Taking the Son Seriously

Dorothy Stang

On February 12, 2005, in the remote regions of the Amazon rain forest, a tiny seventy-four-year-old woman on her way to a land settlement meeting was ambushed by two gunmen. She showed her attackers her Bible, told them that this was the only weapon she possessed, and began to read to them with a clear and radiant voice — with the fervor of a woman who had come to this part of Brazil twenty-one years earlier and had stayed with her people, in spite of numerous death threats. The gunmen watched her for a moment, then they shot her at close range in the head and in the chest and walked away. She died instantly.

Dorothy Stang was dangerous. Many years ago she had walked into the Story and had made it her own. It was, and still is, a story for ordinary people about extraordinary power. It is a story about an ordinary but wonder-filled man who believed that God was his Father and that this same God is our Father too. It is a story that changes anyone who walks into it, and it is dangerous.

The martyrdom of Dorothy Stang filled all of us who knew and loved her with tremendous awe as well as sorrow. It affected many others as well — people who learned about her only through her death. Our hope is that what she stood for in her life (with what appears, on a measuring scale, to have been only minimal success) might be accomplished, ultimately, through her death. That too, after all, is part of the Story she embraced — her story and ours — the extraordinary Christian faith Story. It confronted and threatened the powerful Roman army and procurator some two thousand years ago, when they heard of a healer from Galilee who spoke of and lived the reign of God. It confronted and threatened the government forces in El Salvador who had to deal with a bishop who cared for the poor, with four women and six Jesuit teachers who gave the oppressed of that land help and hope. It confronted and threatened the forces of civil unrest in Liberia when they learned of the return of six nuns (Adorers of the Blood of Christ) who had come back to support and encourage their people during that country's civil strife. It confronted and threatened powerful landowners and loggers in Brazil as they encountered it in a seventy-four-year-old little bit of a woman who stood for the transformation of logging practices and against the deforestation in that country that were destroying the environment and hurting the poor.

Because We Believe

We all, of course, know the Christian Story, *or so we think.* Of late I have come to wonder, however, whether that may in fact be our problem. In my classes on Christian spirituality, therefore (where I always hope that we will encounter the Story anew and allow ourselves to *dare:* dare to dream into it, dare to think big), I have come to wonder out loud with the participants whether, indeed, the world is a better place because of this Story, *because we believe* and our faith can, therefore, bring healing. What is redemption, after all, if it is not utter transformation, and of what value is our personal movement into depth if the world is not touched by it? What if, I ask my students:

- What if God *really* depends on *us* to manifest God's love?
- What if our covenant in Christ is *to be lovers,* that only?
- What if the Supper before he died was all about that covenant, and nothing else?

My work during these, my last years of ministry, has me travel much — giving retreats, workshops, and seminars throughout the world. Everywhere I go, I sense a longing to enter into these kinds of questions, as well as the need for hope — a struggling for the More that religion is at least supposed to point to, if not to give us the opportunity to encounter. This More seems absent today. Fatigue with what used to give life seems to cover the disappointment and, sometimes, the downright cynicism of many. That the assembly is searching desperately for a leader (someone to speak openly of the depth we ache for) but finds none, may perhaps be one explanation for this in a church that "administers" the sacraments and "legislates" what "must be believed" but seems to have little regard for the reality and context of the present moment. Catholicism, even today, seems to prefer replacing dialogue with infallible declarations and chains into silence all those who dare to "wrestle with God," as did Job and Jacob before them and, yes, even Jesus of Nazareth.

Unity in diversity (the Roman Catholic "charism," as Joan Chittister calls it) becomes highly suspect when one experiences a religion mired in the vocabulary of fourth-century Hellenic metaphysics — allowing for no deviation and marginalizing anyone who thinks out of step, that is, beyond the categories of that time.

Most Catholic Christians, along with all Christian fundamentalists, believe that what they are told "has always been believed," and when they cannot so believe any longer — in the light of the context of our time and its changing worldview — they are either silent or they leave. Protestant Christians leave too but seem freer to speak another interpretation or perhaps start yet another church.

The recent arguments about "intelligent design" and the fear of "creationism" illustrate well our situation: If it takes a genius such as Einstein to discover the mathematics of an expanding universe, it ought to be obvious to anyone who *thinks* that "intelligence" somehow is involved in the nature of the universe. Any honest science teacher would most likely mention this commonsense probability to his or her students along with, and not contradictory to, evolution. This action can hardly be said to violate the "separation of church and state." It threatens no one's freedom of scientific research, nor anyone's religion. Yet in today's climate, both possibilities are contemplated by cardinals and judges alike.[1] There is a "staleness" in all of this. "Rigor mortis of the Body" may be a better metaphor, even if it is an excruciating thought. Arrogant declarations of certitude — with one side ridiculing the other — leave the majority of us suffering in confusion and pain.

"Does your view of God build you up?" asks David Steindl-Rast. "Does it give you courage to explore and be creative and make you open and welcoming to those who hold other views? Or does what you have learned about God make you feel worthless, guilty, timid, or skeptical?" One could add other possibilities: tired, de-energized, excluded, antagonistic, disheartened, estranged, and abandoned. "Mystics of all religious traditions," Steindl-Rast mentions in the same reflection, "have glimpsed the same Ultimate Reality that makes each of us whole and all of us one. Yet most God-talk drives us apart."[2]

On Asking the Right Questions

Years ago, on a narrower but not unrelated topic, I suggested reflection on the Arthurian legend of the Fisher King as a way to help religious congregations in their struggle with diminishment. The legend focuses on the need to *ask the right question* in order to gain access to the Holy Grail and free its life-giving powers which, in this story, need to be directed toward the ailing Fisher King and his kingdom. In his travels Parsifal, one of Arthur's knights, finds the Grail in fact already in the Fisher King's possession. Parsifal, however, loses it again when he fails to ask about its purpose. *"Whom does the Grail serve?"* was the crucial question that would have ended his quest in glory and would also have healed his host along with the whole kingdom.[3]

It seems to me that perhaps the dilemma facing our religious questing in Christianity and particularly in Catholicism at this time also revolves around dealing with the wrong issues and failing to ask the right question:

> The legend describes the Fisher king as "being too ill to live, but unable to die." The condition that keeps him this way ... is an inability (perhaps in our age it is an unwillingness, a fear) to ask the right question. And so the Fisher King — *that inner self in all self-aware organisms (be they individual or corporate) that supplies them with energy and life; with meaning, and motive, and vision* — languishes. Oh, the processions are held regularly, and the grail in its splendor is venerated — the symbols and traditions remain, the proper decorum is preserved, the rituals are lovely — but the soul languishes. And the soul is *our soul.*[4]

The soul is the soul of the church. We hear about orthodoxy, holy tradition, and the official teachings of the church, while we (who also read about human development, scientific and medical breakthroughs, church history and the development of dogmatic positions, hermeneutics, exegesis, and so much more) wait for a better day, when more insight will finally be allowed to influence traditional ways of interpretation that no longer empower us in our time.

*Does the world today, in fact,
look or even feel truly redeemed,
and if not, what has gone wrong?*

Catholic bishops talk of the Eucharist as primary to a worshiping church, declare a year for its study and special veneration, and hope for a growth in reverence and awe, while, at the same time, they debate uselessly whether partaking of the Bread of Life is, in fact, a privilege rather than a right. They find themselves justified, therefore, in denying it weekly to thousands, because they prefer a priest shortage of celibates and a God image that finds gender and the sacrament of matrimony a stumbling block to ordination.

Whom does religion serve, and whom does the church that is called to articulate it serve?

On Taking the Son Seriously

A number of years ago I was invited to give a parish mission for a large community in the greater Chicago area. The theme was to be "The Transformation of the Heart," and I was invited to orient the community to this theme during the homily time at all the Sunday liturgies. All the readings were powerful that particular Sunday, but I decided to focus on the Gospel, which happened to tell of the wedding at Cana. A remarkable story, this — perhaps not so much in terms of water transformation as in the role that it assigns to the mother of Jesus as the catalyst for her Son's public ministry. "Do whatever he tells you," Mary quietly instructs the servers at the feast, ignoring her Son's reticence. And when they, in fact, do whatever he asks of them, he saves the party.

A dear priest friend of mine maintains that no scripture story is complete, is in fact of any value, until it becomes

our story — until, as Dorothy Stang did, we *walk into it* and
make it our own. And so I reflected with the parishioners
that day on how much easier it really is to transform water
into wine than to genuinely transform hearts, especially
one's own. The mission of Jesus and our own mission —
because we are baptized into his life and death — is quite
clearly about "heart transformation" and really about nothing else. This requires courage, trust, honesty, and most of
all a sincere willingness on our part. Water transformation
is easy in comparison.

They say that Jesus could not work healing unless there
was trust. That is why, I suppose, after he healed someone,
we hear him say so often, "Go in peace. Your *faith* has
made you whole." Somehow love energies of healer and
wounded soul have to connect for wholeness to happen,
and even the most powerful person can do nothing for us
if our "yes" is being withheld.

That Sunday I told the members of St. Margaret Mary
Parish a beautiful story that I had received over the Inter-
net not long before from a friend of mine. I had no way
of knowing where it had actually originated, but for me
it poignantly identified what the parish was looking for. It
also became the reason for this book, which consciously
started to write itself in me during that parish retreat
experience and continued to haunt me for several years
thereafter:

A wealthy man and his son loved to collect rare works of art.
They had everything in their collection, from Picasso to Raphael,
and would often sit together and admire the great works of art.

Now, when the Vietnam conflict broke out, the son was drafted and went to war. Unfortunately not long into the conflict, while rescuing another soldier, he was killed. The father, of course, was notified of this and grieved deeply.

About a month later, just before Christmas, a young man visited the father. "Sir, you don't know me," he said, "but I am the soldier for whom your son gave his life. He saved many lives that day, and he was carrying me to safety when a bullet struck him in the heart and he died instantly. He often talked about you, and your love for art."

The young man held out a package. "I know this isn't much. I'm not really a great artist," he said, "but I think your son would have wanted you to have this."

The father opened the package. It was a portrait of his son, painted by the young man. He stared in awe at the way the soldier had captured the personality of his son in the painting. The father was so drawn to the eyes that his own eyes welled up with tears. He thanked the young man and offered to pay him for the picture. "Oh, no sir, I could never repay what your son did for me. It's a gift," the young man replied.

The father hung the portrait over his mantle. Every time visitors came to his home he took them to see the portrait of his son before he showed them any of the other great works he had collected.

A few months later the father also died. There was to be a great auction of all his paintings, and many influential people gathered, excited over seeing the great art and having an opportunity to purchase pieces for their collection.

On the platform, for all to see, however, was the painting of the son. The auctioneer pounded his gavel. "We will start the bidding with this picture of the son. Who will bid for this picture?" There was general discontent in the group, and people shouted that they wanted to see the real art, not this simple picture. But the auctioneer seemed determined: "Will someone bid for this painting? Who will start the bidding? $100, $200?" But the crowd wanted the Van Goghs and Rembrandts and seemed to grow angry, shouting for the real bids. Still the auctioneer continued with the painting of the son.

Finally, a voice came from the very back of the room. It was the longtime gardener of the estate. "I'll give $10 for the painting," he offered. Being a poor man, it was all he could afford. "We have $10, who will bid $20?" the auctioneer asked. "Give it to him. Let's see the masters," the crowd shouted. The auctioneer pounded the gavel. "Going once, twice, SOLD for $10," he concluded and then laid down his gavel. "I'm sorry," he told the crowd. "The auction is over."

"What about the paintings?" the crowd wanted to know. "I am sorry," the man repeated. "When I was called to conduct this auction, I was told of a secret stipulation in the will. I was not allowed to reveal that stipulation until this time. Only the painting of the son would be auctioned. Whoever bought that painting would inherit the entire estate, including the paintings, and so, the person who took the son gets everything."

That, I hope, is the theme of this book. God, one could say, "took a major risk" in the divine self-revelation in Jesus two thousand years ago and continues that risk in the call to divinization even today. "Will you take my Son?" God asks us every day, "because, you see, *whoever takes the Son gets everything.*"

Dangerous Memories

That *is* what it is about, really, for all of us. It would seem, though, that often we forget, and even our churches and religious institutions forget or get sidetracked, and then we need each other to bring back the memories. We need time also to reflect and to focus on what these memories actually mean for us today and what, therefore, truly matters in our lives.

His Story is not an easy story — not because it is complicated in its message, but precisely because it is so simple. Doing "whatever he tells us," as Mary admonishes, seems really quite straightforward: "Love one another." "Do good to those who hate you." "Turn the other cheek." "Forgive seventy times seven times." Simple, but, oh, how difficult! Yet in this vision lies our homecoming. We believe that "taking the Son seriously" is how transformation happens both for ourselves and for the world. That is why, for us, *everything depends on it.*

And still the question haunts me and, I believe, it must be asked especially in our time and the present world picture: What does this really mean? Earlier I suggested that we might seriously examine whether the world is indeed a better place because of Jesus Christ and because we believe in his message. Does the world today, in fact, look or even feel truly redeemed, and if not, what has gone wrong? It seems that the time is ripe — for the daring and for those willing to risk having to let go of their own comfort zones — to revisit the memories and the dreams of our ancient faith vision, to do so in hope and with true humility, to question them — trying to contextualize them for our age, asking ourselves, once again, with great serenity but also with total candor:

1. Are our Christian religions truly dynamic, some-how transformative every day? Or have we become complacent in the knowledge:

   - that we are "redeemed,"
   - that all the truths we "need" are contained in our creed forever,
   - that Jesus did whatever he had to do — suffered according to God's will in atonement for our sins, so that there is a "once-and-for-all" to our salvation?

2. Do we belong to a church outside of which there is no salvation or, at best, "difficult" salvation?

3. Can we rest, therefore, on our laurels, provided we do what we are told, believe what we are asked to accept as true — once and for all?

4. And if that is it,

   - What *difference* does it make to the rest of the world?
   - What does all this mean?

5. And if we do not feel comfortable with these prob-ings, how would we want to see things differently?

As I pondered these things over the years, it struck me that perhaps for some of us all this feels like repeating something over and over again, but really *not getting it*. A feeling such as this can be frightening or, at least, disturbing. In the years of my youth, prior to Vatican Council II, everything seemed "taken care of," that is, orderly and neat:

- Salvation was given to me.

- I belonged to a church that had the truth and guaranteed eternal life, provided I followed its precepts.

- The scriptures for many of us gave a historical account of the events of our salvation some two thousand years ago, and of the events of human sin and punishment at the beginning of human history with our first parents in the garden of Eden (an actual place that many of us curiously kept looking for somewhere in the Middle East).

- We talked of the flood, the flight out of Egypt, the Passover event, the star of Bethlehem, the Magi, "no room in the inn," and all the other birth events of Jesus of Nazareth as historical moments.

- What Jesus said and did during his life was taken in its totality as fact.

- The agony in the garden and all subsequent moments of the Passion were biographical to us. We prayed the stations of the cross with fervor and sadness and, with corresponding joy, celebrated the Easter events and all post-resurrection stories.

Only years after the Second Vatican Council did some of us hear (some never did) of such terms as exegesis, hermeneutics, the problem of "proof-texting"; did we learn that mythology can be seen as a legitimate form of religious language and communication, that scripture is in many respects literature, a good portion of which contains myth and needs to be understood that way.

When one studies theology today in universities where scripture research has become thoroughly ecumenical, the scholarly approach to scripture and the theology based on it is, of course, taken for granted. What puzzles me, however, is the fact that among ordinary Christians, and many homilists as well, it is being recognized much less clearly and with enormous reticence. Few among our young and even our ageing and often well-educated adults are *informed* believers. When consciously confronted with the major contradictions of non-contextualized Catholicism in particular, and Christianity in general, some simply leave their religion. Others seem to "defect in place":[5] They "stay in the church" but refuse to give these issues the thought they deserve; they continue to get married and have their children baptized in their religion of origin without much other involvement. They may also privately reject some official and even "dogmatized" interpretations of their religion, close their ears during Sunday homilies, and stop paying attention to ecclesial dicta. Still others simply refuse to situate their religious beliefs in the present moment. They feverishly hold on to unprocessed religion — the "body of faith." They proselytize or condemn others who do not, exhibiting fervor and the outdated religious chauvinism of "true" believers, without thought.

What is it, for example, that makes a highly educated professor of literature incapable of connecting with his own discipline when approaching the Gospels? He asks why Jesus said what he did in the garden of Gethsemane, or why God would have chosen crucifixion as the act of atonement. He sees these events as purely historical renditions and, in that respect (in spite of his advanced education), is not too different from the economically and educationally deprived woman attending a support group for victims of domestic violence who wonders whether the God who willed the crucifixion of his Son might not be a child abuser.

What is it, perhaps most disturbing of all, that has a film such as Mel Gibson's *The Passion of the Christ* attract such crowds of believers with such devotion, and with such insistence on restitution and on personal atonement for inherited sins? What was it, in the first place, that had Mel Gibson take the interpretations of a nineteenth-century writer (without apparently any consideration of subsequent scholarship) and present a sadistic horror for religious edification, dismissing anyone who could not stomach the gore as unwilling to face the reality of his or her redemption? Why are so many believers in Christ seemingly so afraid of Christ's freedom? Why are explorations into other possibilities of faith interpretation, into more contemporary reflections, perhaps, on the events we call salvation history, so often treated with scorn?

During the question period after a lecture I gave recently on this topic to some four hundred pastoral ministers in Los Angeles, a woman reflected sadly that the opportunity to explore questions of the faith is simply denied even to pastoral ministers. "We think these thoughts privately," she observed, "but have no forum to process them to-gether." Theology is useless unless it can be transmitted to the body of the faithful in language that clarifies rather than obfuscates, that speaks to present-day reality rather than to a worldview and reality no longer relevant. The power of Christianity is tested in the hearts it reaches and the transformation it effects.

And so today we ask once again: Whom does religion serve and whom does the church that is called to articulate it serve?

1. How can we today meaningfully appropriate God's love blossoming forth to the fullest in Christ Jesus, as we believe, and poured out completely in the events that we celebrate as our redemption?

2. What response can we give to this creative love of God in *our* time and place, in this *our* culture and the conditions of *our* present moment? In other words:

+ How do we today say yes to this kind of love, and

+ Can we?

3. What does it mean for us to be covenanted to the Christ, to "take up the cross," to be resurrection people today, for our culture, and for all of creation?

I write this book because the old answers to these questions no longer "speak to my soul," disturbing as this may be for a Catholic who was well trained to listen and obey. There is a languishing (not too different, I suspect, from the languishing of the Fisher King), and I am struggling for greater depth. My hope is that you, the reader, are with me in this struggle, and that the energy generated through our probing will bring genuine healing for us all.

Thoughts and Questions for Meditation

What are your thoughts concerning the following selections from chapter 1?

1. We all, of course, know the Christian Story, *or so we think*. Of late I have come to wonder, however, whether *that* may in fact be our problem. In my classes on Christian spirituality, therefore, I have come to wonder out loud with the participants whether, indeed, the world is a better place because of this Story, *because we believe*, and our faith can, therefore, bring healing. What is redemption, after all, if it is not utter transformation, and of what value is our personal movement into depth if the world is not touched by it?

2. What if God *really* depends on *us* to manifest God's love? What if our covenant in Christ is *to be lovers*, that only? What if the Supper before he died was all about that covenant, and nothing else?

3. Most Catholic Christians, along with all Christian fundamentalists, believe that what they are told "has always been believed," and, when they cannot so believe any longer — in the light of the context of our time and its changing worldview — they are either silent or they leave.

4. Does your view of God build you up? Does it give you courage to explore and be creative and make you open

and welcoming to those who hold other views? Or does what you have learned about God make you feel worthless, guilty, timid, skeptical, tired, de-energized, excluded, antagonistic, disheartened, estranged, and abandoned. Mystics of all religious traditions have glimpsed the same Ultimate Reality that makes each of us whole and all of us one. *Yet most God-talk drives us apart.*

5. It seems to me that perhaps the dilemma facing our religious questing in Christianity and particularly in Catholicism at this time also revolves around dealing with the wrong issues and failing to ask the right question. Catholic bishops talk of the Eucharist as primary to a worshiping church, declare a year for its study and special veneration, and hope for a growth in reverence and awe, while, at the same time, they debate uselessly whether partaking of the Bread of Life is, in fact, a privilege rather than a right. They find themselves justified, therefore, in denying it weekly to thousands because they prefer a priest shortage of celibates and a God image that finds gender and the sacrament of matrimony a stumbling block to ordination. *Whom does religion serve, and whom does the church that is called to articulate it serve?*

6. No scripture story is complete, is in fact of any value, until it becomes *our story* — until, as Dorothy Stang did, we *walk into it* and *make it our own.*

7. His Story is not an easy story — not because it is complicated in its message, but precisely because it

is so simple. Doing "whatever he tells us," as Mary admonishes, seems really quite straightforward: "Love one another." "Do good to those who hate you." "Turn the other cheek." "Forgive seventy times seven times." Simple, but, oh, how difficult! Yet in this vision lies our homecoming.

8. The mission of Jesus and our own mission — because we are baptized into his life and death — is quite clearly about "heart transformation" and really about nothing else.

9. What are your thoughts regarding the concluding questions of this chapter?

❦ T W O ❦

Primordial Faith

A Quest for the Holy

To head toward a star — this only.
— Martin Heidegger

Wilderness Replete with Light

We live in extraordinary times: On the one hand we experience unprecedented darkness, confusion, violence, and war; on the other hand creativity and insights abound. I have mentioned often, and do so wherever I go, that there is a transformation of consciousness emerging among us (sometimes almost in spite of us and in the face of great fear and resistance) and calling us to responsible stewardship.

As anyone interested in human evolution and spiritual development will know, I am not the only one observing this. Nor is this a recent phenomenon, although the quantity of studies on, and the number of diverse disciplines interested in, this topic has certainly grown considerably of late. From His Holiness the Dalai Lama to consciousness pioneer Ken Wilber, human potential and self-development expert Wayne W. Dyer, physicists

David Bohm, Fritjof Capra, and Arthur Sajonc, cosmol-
ogist Brian Swimme, psychiatrist Stanislav Groff, philosopher and physicist Danah Zohar, social scientist Diarmuid
Ó Murchú, theologian and biblical scholar Walter Wink,
and many, many more, the word is out that human potential far exceeds our wildest dreams, and that we are being
propelled forward from the roots of our very being into
depths of consciousness and insight hitherto unfathomed.

In this time, then, of turmoil and confusion as well as
of such immense promise, I believe that the roles of both
religion and authentic spirituality need to be reexamined
and perhaps situated anew. I am convinced that both can
and need to play a major part in helping us respond to
our innate search for meaning in the midst of chaos and
of a life often devoid of purpose and significance. They
need to support us as we plumb the depth to which this
age, humanity itself, and the universe as a whole are calling us — a depth of which we are capable and for which
we are, therefore, responsible. Their task, however, will not
be easy. Years of entrenchment (1) in archaic worldviews,
(2) in the metaphysics of ancient cultures that has long
ago lost its vitality, (3) in bureaucracy (its structures of
domination, of useless control over and attempts to manipulate fields of learning and research not in its purview), and
(4) in the inability or unwillingness to own mistakes and
advocate change — all have rendered religious organizations and the organized religions they represent top-heavy
and ineffective.

To provide necessary support in the human quest for the
Holy, then, it would seem that what is asked of religions

today, perhaps more so than at any other time in history, is the courage to let go of certitudes and longtime answers that perhaps served them well in the past but now can no longer respond to the questions that are emerging. What is asked of all of us who adhere to any organized religion is acceptance of, and reconciliation with, change and tentativeness. We know today that complete and final answers simply are not ours to expect. Our peace and our homecoming are *in the journey.* What is asked of us is trust that, in fact, all through the ages the Spirit has been present and will continue to unfold in our time and context as well. A desperate need for courage, authenticity, and honesty is upon us.

Focusing the Issue

To avoid confusion and hopefully to clear away the debris of centuries of categorization and institutionalism, let me begin by identifying my take on terms that many of us use interchangeably to describe our religious involvement. Of particular interest to me are words such as "faith," "spirituality," and "religion" (organized religion, in particular). Many of us do not differentiate these and subsume one under the other in various and often inconsistent ways.

When we reject an interpretation of God that is offered by our religion, for example, we tend to see this as "losing" our faith. We speak of "having to believe" certain things if we are Catholics, for example, and treat faith as an obligatory response to the teachings of our religion. For many of us, faith and religion are therefore interchangeable and, whereas this has become part of common parlance, it can, in many respects, also deprive us of depth experiences in our quest for the Holy. These, if we consider them at all, we quite frequently relegate to a vague notion of spirituality that, among other rarely identified things, somehow involves believing in a higher power and being kind to people. "She doesn't belong to a religion," we say, "but she is spiritual." There seems to be much confusion in all of this.

It could be said, perhaps, that, consciously or not, the various organized religions have taken hold of and swallowed up what quite possibly can exist in its own right and belongs to experiences that can be prior to or independent of institutionalization. I offer some possible distinctions and clarifications here, not from the point of view of academic nitpicking (where I would probably fail), but in the hope of freeing experience, expanding the field of religious encounter, and broadening our sense of the pure and simple holiness that is human existence in its original intent.

In Search of the Self

Some years ago I taught a course in Christian anthropology at the seminary in Cincinnati. My students nicknamed the course "Fiand's 'Who Am I?' class," primarily because we always started the quarter by exploring this question to its uncomfortable depths — challenging ourselves to probe beyond the functional responses of name, occupation, affiliation, etc., that we so glibly give to it, and by which we "firm up" our identity.

We wanted to discover and experience that the "I" that I am (my deepest self, not my ego) can, in fact, never find within itself — within its achievements and concrete history — the reason for its own existence. We wanted to come to the realization (even though the classroom setting in its artificiality and relative comfort would rob us somewhat of the reality of authentic and often painful life experience) that for each of us our identity is not in what we do, what our positions, nationalities, backgrounds, degrees, etc., are. We wanted to come to grips with the frustration and confusion that ensue when the inability to answer who we really are moves us almost desperately into the *why* of our existence that for so many of us seems useless if it cannot be answered by what we do, by our achievements, or even the lack thereof: *If my being is not explained by what I do, by my vocation to be a mother, a father, a writer, a priest, a doctor or nurse who spends her or his days healing, a statesman or stateswoman serving his or her country, a soldier defending her or his country, then who am I really, and why am I here?* We wanted to get to the point of helplessness, to the emptiness, as well as to the mystery that has us meet ourselves beyond or before all expectations — met or unmet. We wanted to feel the hollowness, the "gap," that Thomas Merton talks about, in the hope that from there perhaps the primitive awareness of finitude might blossom forth, and we could experience Kierkegaard's "leap into the absurd," discover the "More" that William James points to and we already referred to in the previous chapter, the More that holds us and yet is beyond all of us and seems to elude us so often.

Somehow, because of our inability to touch our deepest identity by way of the "objectifiable" data of our own making and to find stability there, certain options seem to present themselves to us: We can "opt out," as did the nihilists of the twentieth century. We can, in other words, despair of meaning, reject its possibility, and declare life to be absurd: If we cannot find the reason for our being here within ourselves or, for that matter, in other humans — our parents, ancestors, nation, etc. — there is no reason, and therefore life must be absurd.

Primary Faith

The other option is the Kierkegaardian "leap" mentioned already: one moves beyond logic toward accepting a greater reality, beyond human power in itself (though, paradoxically, it is nevertheless found deep "within") as the source of meaning, of the mystery that is "I." That reality, as many of us know, Aquinas of old would say, "we call God": If I cannot find the reason for my being here within myself or in other humans, there must be something or someone greater (a force, potential, energy) that holds me in being and knows why.

"Only when there is nothing left for us to speculate about," I wrote during those teaching years at the seminary, when "the encounter with the depth of our humanity has rendered us utterly speechless, is there appropriate room for the all-encompassing embrace of the Holy One. Only then, be it in ecstasy or in agony, are we opened to the radical experience of ourselves as pointers into the mystery, no more and no less."[1] The process of the "Who Am I?" journey, I explained to my classes, is of course not at all clear or easy and is often abandoned only to be picked up again later. As Rahner wrote many years ago, "This primitive, nameless, and themeless experience is apparently wholly repressed and buried by our daily routine, by all that we otherwise have to do."[2] Nor is there any "guarantee that, once surfaced and probed, it cannot at some point 'be buried again even through our theological, ascetic, and pious chatter.'"[3] Nevertheless, along with Sebastian Moore, I believe that this question, however it might be asked and however often repeated, is, indeed, mystical at its root — one of the deepest and certainly one of the most fundamental religious questions we wrestle with. And it is *here,* I believe, where we can locate our "primary faith" experience.

In a homily on a recent feast of the Epiphany, the presider started his reflection by referencing Scott Peck's book *The Road Less Traveled.* He observed that, were he to write a book, he would not start it with "Life is hard," as did Peck, but would, instead, observe, "Everyone is looking for something." The star that lured the Magi, he said, symbolizes that "something" — the *beyond us,* the *greater than we are* that we have been reflecting on. We search and long for it, as the Magi symbolized, with a hunger that is endemic to the human condition as a whole. Karl Rahner would see this hunger as an inbuilt grace that gifts us all, regardless of religion or culture, and that has done so from the beginning of our existence. It pursues us, as did Francis

Thompson's Hound of Heaven, and leaves us dissatisfied at the core until we surrender to our poverty and want and thus allow it to surface.

"The one we are looking for," someone once said, "is the one looking." We are, in Martin Heidegger's words, "gazed upon" and have been from the beginning. This initial luring, this invitation to plunge into the Mystery that haunts all of us in various forms — even unrecognized ones — throughout our life, and that ultimately offers us the possibility of accepting the More, is therefore primordial. The *yes* response that it invites is *prior* (in nature, though not always in time) to any deductive reasoning, and seems more a matter of intuition and feeling than systematic thought. It is primitive, a depth *yes*, "primary faith" — first, not always, as I said, on the temporal level, for it can become conscious sometimes only late in life, and out of deep human yearning. I understand it as our initial, as well as our foundational (underlying) surrender to ultimate meaning in the midst of experiencing the mystery, suffering, and chaos of life.

What I am presenting here as "faith," therefore, is not first and foremost the acceptance of a particular creed, even though we are accustomed to thinking of faith that way. Because of the pervasiveness of the Christian religion, especially in the West, faith, as I mentioned already, has been linked to creed, whereas the primal *yes* to depth is neglected and can even conveniently be relegated to the "secular" sphere, for example, as "peak experiences" and philosophical wonder. Creeds, however, are really on a different plane and come much later. Primary faith precedes creeds and does not have to lead to them, although it can, and often does. It can, however, also be hampered and even destroyed by creeds. Primary faith cannot be recited, nor programmed, nor declared with *ex cathedra* statements. It is rather a depth intuition that grips us — sometimes over and over again — and has done so in numerous ways from the beginning of the human phenomenon.[4] It is our positive response to wonder filled with awe in the face of mystery — the response to the awe, in other words, that emerges out of wonder.

Spirituality

I want to identify authentic spirituality as manifesting itself primarily in our response to this depth intuition. In our time it also helps return us to this intuition when religion has abandoned us. I see it as addressing our depth quest for the More, as present among us, along with the primordial faith experience, since our early beginnings in Neanderthal and Paleolithic times.[5] "Spirituality concerns an ancient and primal search for meaning," says Ó Murchú, "that is as old as humanity itself and . . . belongs — as an inherent energy — to the evolutionary unfolding of creation itself."[6]

Religion, as we understand it today in its organized structure, along with the theology that articulates and explains it, came much later (by thousands of years) than what we are describing here, even though the words "faith," "spirituality," and "religion" are not always differentiated clearly and are often used interchangeably.[7]

Spirituality is grounded in thirst and fire, in the shared intuition of the Mystery, not primarily in organization and
categorization. It responds to the wonder-filled *yes* of primordial faith as an all-encompassing phenomenon, gives
it a home, and symbolizes it, embodies it, ritualizes it in
dance, art, and music, grows it, and cultivates it.

Anne Carr, to whom I feel greatly indebted whenever
I write or speak on this topic, says it well when she
points out that spirituality "reaches into our unconscious
or half-conscious depths. And while it shapes behavior and
attitude, it is really more than a conscious moral code. In
relation to God, it is who we really are, the deepest self, not
entirely accessible to our comprehensive self-reflection"[8]
and, I would add, always open to further growth and
evolution. Our spirituality, if you will, is ever pervaded,
therefore, by the Mystery that is our quest, as well as the
mystery that we are.

Carr warns, however, that, in some respects, spirituality can be taken for granted, "remain for the most part
unexamined, resting on convention, upbringing, or social
expectations."[9] Its original impulse can also at times be in-
hibited along with our questing, especially when answers
are given definitively, and rituals become codified — resting on an "un-reflected" past and on arbitrary and outdated
church law. Our spiritual hunger, then, remains for the
most part unaddressed — even unconscious — though it
does not cease to permeate our lives.

Spirituality is somewhat like the air we breathe. It surrounds us and flows through us. It is the ambience, the
flavor, the touch, the "feel" of our lives. We live and move

in the context of our spirituality. Out of it we identify our loves, our fears, our hatreds, what we accept and what we reject. I mention often that we even hug and party in the context of our spirituality. We interpret the world — what we see as noble, how we understand our place in the world, how we relate to God, the value of life, the inevitability and meaning of death, issues related to the dignity of the human person, of nature, and of all creation — in the context of our spirituality. By way of example, we could say that the "Abba" of Jesus came from his spirituality, as did his style of prayer that flowed from the Abba experience, as did his concern for justice, as did his power for healing and raising from the dead. He expressed through these his intimacy with the Holy, his all-pervasive sense of the sacred and of love.

The Patriarchal Father, on the other hand, came from the religion that was formulated in Christianity years later and tried somehow to capture and organize this vision of Jesus for the culture which it was evangelizing and to which it, in many respects, belonged — the Roman and Hellenic culture of the day. Enculturation is, of course, unavoidable and even necessary. In the Christian tradition, however, it seems to have ended sometime around the fourth century, when the Hellenic worldview (cosmology and metaphysics) became calcified in official doctrinal statements, declared to be unchanging and definitive forever.

And that was, and continues to be, the problem. It is really quite difficult to "organize" and define spirituality and vision without doing violence to its inspiration. In

times of change (and history is full of these) and in moments of crisis and confusion that is what often happens.
We feel the ground slipping from beneath our feet, and
we want to hold on and to stay in control. And so we
organize and define (that is, put limits around) what first
moved freely within us, flowed out of us, and motivated
our action. We also dismiss, with varying degrees of harsh-
ness, what does not fit into the pattern we so painstakingly
created for our God experience.

In the old days we had witch hunts against those who
honored creation and studied the secrets of the earth. We
divided the world into realms for the spirit and realms for
matter. The earth, its herbs and fruits, in spite of their
healing power, belonged to the material realm and were to
be avoided because we saw them as remote from God, the
supreme Spirit, who alone could heal. We had inquisitions
for those who did not agree with our interpretation of the
world and decided that "error" had no rights. We tortured
dissenters because they did not understand the Mystery on
our terms (as if anyone could understand it anyway). They
were different and, therefore, they threatened us.

Today they still do. But today, although we uphold the
obligatory nature of dogmas and doctrines and even of
mere magisterial viewpoints, we do not have the same
power of enforcement. We silence, deny communion,
try to legislate oaths of allegiance, and ostracize those
we would have previously burned at the stake. We find
catchwords, also, such as "New Age" and "modernity"
or "postmodernity." We attach everything that cannot be
organized or that we cannot understand or that we find

threatening to these terms, and dismiss it — everything that uses new ways of seeing, different categories of approach to the Mystery of life. The Mystery, of course, still pervades the universe as it has always done, but in various ways it has been safely "domesticated" by us over the years.

This Mystery, however, speaks to our deepest longing and hunger, our wonder and awe. And because it defies formulation, definition, official clarification, and control, it often withers in our churches where we claim we "possess" it, and where fewer and fewer opportunities exist to look more deeply, to dialogue openly, to explore and wonder, to express longing, intuition, and reverence for that which defies explanation and regulation — that which requires surrender, humility, and the acceptance of human inadequacy, even papal and magisterial inadequacy.

Religion

As I see it, religion, at its best, is the articulated response by the community to the depth quest experienced and intuited in primordial faith and affirmed, internalized, as well as symbolized, in spirituality. Religion cannot be cut off from that depth quest and remain authentic. It is, in other words, not primary, but that does not mean it is not important. It is, in fact, very important, but comes second to what precedes it in human openness to the Mystery. When it usurps the primary position, it betrays its task.

Religion, to be sure, is *grounded* in the original intuition of a religious genius — Jesus, the Buddha, Muhammad. It attempts to speak the vision, to formulate it for the culture in what might best be summarized as *word* (that is, holy scripture, sacred documents), *code* (that is, moral norms embraced by the community), and *cult* (ritual and worship for the community gathered in prayer). Religion has a very important role, therefore, wherever people come together in community and are looking for inspiration and guidance in their common quest for meaning.

But religion cannot replace spirituality without itself withering, because the freedom, the fire, and the light in religion come from spirituality. Without them religion tends to become stale, rule-bound, and fixated. Without spirituality, as in fact the word indicates, religion loses its spirit, its energy. Because spirituality is "our deepest self in relation to God, to the whole, and so literally to everything, it changes [and] grows, ... in the whole context of life."[10] Infallibility and permanence are foreign to it. It can, if you will, (and is meant to) "role with the punches" — with the context and experiences of the times. Because it is guided, first and foremost, by the quest for deep meaning opened up by primordial faith and not primarily by fixed religious interpretations or cultic expressions, it has the power (if it is allowed a place in the community and can, therefore, be brought to consciousness) to respond creatively to the changing worldview.

We might say, by way of example, that it is primarily spirituality today that is fascinated by the discoveries of science in quantum theory and astrophysics. It is spirituality, also, that wants to explore other religious traditions and ancient practices for their "wisdom," including "woman wisdom," that may be helpful to the over-rationalistic culture of Western religion: Reiki, methods of healing touch, aboriginal practices, even shamanism — their respect for the human body and reverence for all of creation, their contact with energy, light, and the realm of the spirit world. Spirituality wants to find a place for both ancient and new discoveries in its own God quest. Because it is not interested in power and control over others, it can do this with wonder, with gratitude for the insights of humankind throughout the ages, with awe, and with an ever evolving awareness of God's revelation in the here and now. In so doing, it can provide energy to religion, help it to transcend its strictures, to grow also, become pastoral in crisis situations, retrieve its ancient, life-giving charism, and, when necessary, transcend the Law as, in fact, Jesus did — picking corn on the Sabbath and expanding the experience of covenant beyond Jewish ritual into the table fellowship that became Christian Eucharist.

And that, more than anything else, is why religion needs spirituality today and the connection to the primary faith experience. Religion has a necessary tendency toward structure, stability, and control in its attempts to stay connected to the religious genius of its founding tradition — what that person said and did. To be sure, it uses theology to contextualize and explain its formulations in time and place, but it likes stability and values tradition and, therefore, the past — frequently, as history shows, at the expense of the present and the future. This tendency, clearly, does not prove helpful in a time of necessary change and paradigm shifts such as ours. The more structured a religion tends to be, the harder it finds giving a creative, non-threatened, and non-threatening response to change, and the more it tries to retrench and hold on for the sake of what it sees as permanent by God's decree.

What Is Asked of Religion Today?

Ours are, without question, turbulent and changing times: our national and religious values are in many respects under siege both from within and from without. One can, therefore, easily get the feeling that everything is falling apart. Cynicism and despair seem rampant among us in both the old and the young, and the question could easily be asked: Where is God in all of this? Where is the good, really?

As I mentioned already, however, light does seem to appear through the clouds. New insights and discoveries abound and are being proclaimed everywhere. "God is not absent but in our very midst," we are being told by those who study these insights. They call us to responsible stewardship and assure us that we are gifted with everything it takes to be creative stewards of this world.

Science, in many of its disciplines, is today beginning to acknowledge mystery, pointing us to the elegance of creation and calling us to respect and reverence. Its discoveries are pointing unquestionably to our interdependence and inviting us to deepen our sense of community, recognizing that our boundaries are cracking. We are beginning to experience communion — not just among humans but, amazingly, with all of creation. We are beginning to take it seriously that we are cosmically interconnected. Nothing happens anywhere in the universe that does not affect everything everywhere instantly. The notion that no one is an island has become a scientific fact. The mechanistic approach to creation is being challenged, as well, and we are being invited to see the world as a living, breathing, ever changing and transforming universe with hidden and mysterious principles of order and mind.

These insights call for a new depth response: What may appear at first to undermine tradition and creed needs to be explored for relevance to contemporary religion. Old and unchanging laws not only need to be reappraised but also to be integrated and rethought — and that within a faith system that has preached permanence ever since it accepted the Greek worldview centuries ago, which abhors change as fickle and unreliable, and which has created dogmas to assure solidity and declare infallibility. This is a mammoth task!

What is asked of spirituality today, therefore, is courage and perseverance in its quest for deeper insight. What is asked of religion is an acceptance of the fact that it needs spirituality more than ever: to keep it anchored in the depth quest; to keep it questing, in fact, rather than sitting on the truth it thinks it owns; to keep it focused on the essentials of the gospel objective to be about the reign of God. We have had ample evidence through the years, and especially lately, that religion's concern for justice can easily atrophy to concern for upholding existing structures and the positions of power that flow from them. Its concern for tradition can readily hide behind old ways of understanding our relationship with God and the world that have been dogmatized for the sake of permanence and that no longer fit.

If my being is not explained by what I do, by my vocation to be a mother, a father, a writer, a priest, a doctor or nurse, then who am I really, and why am I here?

What is asked of religion, therefore, is to let go of answers that no longer respond to questions; to accept change and possibility rather than fixate on interpretations that came from another worldview and were profitable then, but have lost all significance today. Since, science assures us, there really is nothing permanent except change, religion will do well to trust that the Spirit of God continues to unfold in our midst, that creation and redemption are ongoing, and that the Christ event has resources up to now untapped and is calling us to new ways of understanding hitherto unheard of.

The reign of God — the only reason for our existence, the only purpose for church and our faith life in general — is calling us to major concerns beyond our own hierarchical structures of power. Worrying about precedence in worship and ritual, about who can come into the sanctuary, touch the sacred vessels and when, receive communion or be denied (if this is even justified in the light of how Jesus behaved) clearly is secondary to being about feeding the worshipers, educating and empowering God's people. Fascination with the past does not justify ignoring the intellectual and spiritual needs of the present. God does not abandon God's creation, but I cannot at times help wondering whether God might not be utterly bored with what the religious establishment of our time considers important and upset with what it so often does not concern itself.

A number of years ago I came upon a book by Petru Dumitriu in which he reflected on what I think many of us and certainly those with whom we minister "in the trenches" have to face each day. He dedicated the book "To

the Unknown God," and I cannot help wanting to ask religion today how well it knows this God, or whether in fact
it realizes how this God sees the world where witnessing
to the gospel is all that matters. I wonder how our understanding of what is important or unimportant matches
what this God classifies as important or unimportant, as
good or as evil. This is what Dumitriu had to say:

> Evil is working from ten to twelve hours a day; it is
> child labor, back-breaking work, the agonizing task,
> the workaholic obsession — all Evil. Unemployment
> at the same time as Butter Mountains — Himalayas
> of butter kept in store and going bad to the tune
> of millions, Everests of jam flushed down the drain,
> cattle killed off . . . and thrown into a common bone
> yard to keep prices up.
>
> The laws of free trade and the Common Market
> praised to high heaven (while millions die of starva-
> tion in the Sahara, in Bengal or the Horn of Africa)
> and extolled by people who keep our noses to the
> grindstone so that we can pay our taxes — those taxes
> with which they finance the destruction of the fruits
> of our labors — yes, that is what Evil is. Evil is all
> that is stupid, and the joyful acceptance of stupidity
> by those who profit by it, and by those who do not
> suffer because of it.[11]

I went back to that reading a few days after the attacks
on the World Trade Center and the Pentagon. As horrible
as those acts of terrorism were against America and, indeed, against the entire Western world, and in spite of the

sorrow and grief we all feel, I could not help wondering whether the evil we all witnessed on September 11, 2001, the evil that has been our response, and the evil described by Petru Dimitriu were not somehow linked. The will to power is a terrible thing at any time, but when, regardless of what side of the conflict we now find ourselves on, it uses Christianity or Islam as a subterfuge, it becomes diabolical (*dia-bolo* — to tear apart).

Religion needs to witness to the God who seems to have become "un-known" in our time, in spite of all the talk of liberation. We cannot afford to stand by in silence when hatred and confusion violate our heritage. We have to go deep within ourselves and speak the Christ vision, or our religion has lost its flavor and becomes irrelevant. "Our fundamental error as Christians," says Jack Nelson-Pallmeyer, "is that we allow the biblical word to conform to the dominant culture and thereby rob it of its capacity for liberation. This helps explain why most Christians and churches in the United States are indifferent to or ignorant of the war against the poor."[12]

As Christians we know that our "Charter Story" speaks eloquently to all of this. It is difficult for me to imagine that it is possible to ignore it so, let alone misinterpret and manipulate it to our advantage! Was not Jesus himself a victim of the empire because of his message of hope? And that precisely may be the point — he was a victim, and that is frightening. It is easier to "administer" the faith than to speak its message with our lives. We have, I believe, become top-heavy "administering" it. We need leadership in living its vision and, if need be, dying for it.

Thoughts and Questions for Meditation

What are your thoughts concerning the following selections from chapter 2?

1. Years of entrenchment (1) in archaic worldviews, (2) in the metaphysics of ancient cultures that has long ago lost its vitality, (3) in bureaucracy (its structures of domination, of useless control over and attempts to manipulate fields of learning and research not in its purview), and (4) in the inability or unwillingness to own mistakes and advocate change — all have rendered religious organizations and the organized religions they represent top-heavy and ineffective.

2. What is asked of all of us who adhere to any organized religion is acceptance of, and reconciliation with, change and tentativeness. We know today that complete and final answers simply are not ours to expect. Our peace and our homecoming are in the journey. What is asked of us is trust that, in fact, all through the ages the Spirit has been present and will continue to unfold in our time and context as well. A desperate need for courage, authenticity, and honesty is upon us.

3. The "I" that I am (my deepest self, not my ego) can, in fact, never find within itself — within its achievements and concrete history — the reason for its own existence.

4. If my being is not explained by what I do, by my vocation to be a mother, a father, a writer, a priest, a doctor, or nurse who spends her or his days healing, a

statesman or stateswoman serving his or her country, a soldier defending her or his country, then who am I really, and why am I here?

5. "The one we are looking for," said Francis of Assisi, "is the one looking." We are, in Martin Heidegger's words, "gazed upon" and have been from the beginning. This initial luring, this invitation to plunge into the Mystery that haunts all of us in various forms — even unrecognized ones — throughout our life, and that ultimately offers us the possibility of accepting the More, is therefore primordial. The *yes* response that it invites is *prior* (in nature, though not always in time) to any deductive reasoning. . . . It is primitive, a depth *yes*, "primary faith" — first, not always, as I said, on the temporal level, for it can become conscious, sometimes, only late in life, and out of deep human yearning. I understand it as our initial, as well as our foundational (underlying) surrender to ultimate meaning in the midst of experiencing the mystery, suffering, and chaos of life.

6. What I am presenting here as "faith" is not first and foremost the acceptance of a particular creed, even though we are accustomed to think of faith that way. Creeds are really on a different plane and come much later. Primary faith precedes creeds and does not have to lead to them, although it can, and often does. It can, however, also be hampered and even destroyed by creeds. Primary faith cannot be recited, nor programmed, nor declared with *ex cathedra* statements.

It is our positive response to wonder filled with awe in the face of mystery — the response to the awe, in other words, that emerges out of wonder.

7. Spirituality is grounded in thirst and fire, in the shared intuition of the Mystery, not primarily in organization and categorization. It responds to the wonder-filled *yes* of primordial faith as an all-encompassing phenomenon, gives it a home, and symbolizes it, embodies it, ritualizes it in dance, art, and music, grows it, and cultivates it.

8. The "Abba" of Jesus came from his spirituality, as did his style of prayer that flowed from the Abba experience, as did his concern for justice, as did his power for healing and raising from the dead. He expressed through these his intimacy with the Holy, his all-pervasive sense of the sacred and of love.

9. The Patriarchal Father came from the religion that was formulated in Christianity years later and tried somehow to capture and organize this vision of Jesus for the culture which it was evangelizing and to which it, in many respects, belonged — the Roman and Hellenic culture of the day.

10. As I see it, religion, at its best, is the articulated response by the community to the depth quest experienced and intuited in primordial faith and affirmed, internalized, as well as symbolized, in spirituality. Religion cannot be cut off from that depth quest and remain authentic. It is, in other words, not primary, but that does not mean it is not important. It is, in

fact, very important but comes second to what precedes it in human openness to the Mystery. When it usurps the primary position, it betrays its task.

11. Spirituality wants to find a place for both ancient and new discoveries in its own God quest. Because it is not interested in power and control over others, it can do this with wonder, with gratitude for the insights of humankind throughout the ages, with awe, and with an ever evolving awareness of God's revelation in the here and now. In so doing, it can provide energy to religion, help it to transcend its strictures, to grow also, become pastoral in crisis situations, retrieve its ancient, life-giving charism, and when necessary transcend the Law as, in fact, Jesus did — picking corn on the Sabbath and expanding the experience of covenant beyond Jewish ritual into the table fellowship that became Christian Eucharist.

12. What is asked of spirituality today, therefore, is courage and perseverance in its quest for deeper insight. What is asked of religion is an acceptance of the fact that it needs spirituality more than ever: to keep it anchored in the depth quest; to keep it questing, in fact, rather than sitting on the truth it thinks it owns; to keep it focused on the essentials of the gospel objective to be about the reign of God.

❦ THREE ❦

Situating Ourselves

You know that, among the Gentiles, rulers lord it over their subjects, and the great make their authority felt. It shall not be so with you; among you, whoever wants to be great must be your servant, and whoever wants to be first, must be the slave of all. — Matthew 20:25–27

Community — A Vision for Our Time

In a beautiful reflection on the leading question that preoccupied Pierre Teilhard de Chardin throughout his life, Beatrice Bruteau describes for us Teilhard's "primary faith" response: "For our lives to be meaningful, they must succeed in continuing the creative work of evolution."[1] Teilhard saw evolution as a movement, taking place through the "creative unions" of simple elements in creation, attracted to each other in terms of their "characteristic energies" and because of "their natural affinity," and joining together toward greater complexity and higher consciousness. Subatomic particles come together to form atoms. These unite to create molecules which, in turn, unite to form cells, and they, primitive organisms, etc. Something new, more complex, and more conscious, therefore,

62

emerges from the union of the less complex, and less conscious.[2]

For Teilhard, creation is progression, with ever greater interiority and self-possession, toward *community*. It comes about (by way of attraction and out of the necessity to evolve) through a process of self-gift toward union and for the sake of greater consciousness. The movement is at first brought about simply by the evolutionary intent itself until eventually, in us, human consciousness allows for recognition, and our self-awareness and freedom invite us to enter this process and say *yes* to its integrity. In this way, the possibility opens up for us to become "the uniting elements" that further evolution and upon whom it depends.

Bruteau warns, however, that, "at this point evolution meets a situation that is unique in its history [since] the uniting elements in our case are free agents. We will not automatically unite merely because of some natural affinity." Human consent is a crucial factor now, and therefore, because we are free, "we can each choose whether we will enter into the proposed union or not. Thus the union, the new being, the next creative advance in evolution, will come about only if we freely consent to form it. This is why Teilhard says that the whole cosmic enterprise now hangs on our decision: *we are evolution*."[3]

Teilhard identifies as *love* the creative energy that we hold in common — the *human* energy that would allow for us to be drawn together, that calls us therefore toward union. Human energy is not just physical, or chemical, or biological. "It is the energy of thinking, or knowing, and the energy of loving, or willing. It is this most intimate energy of ours that we are asked to commit to the new union."[4]

Donald Nichol, in his classic little book *Holiness*, thinks along these same lines when he describes the movement throughout creation as inherent "self-sacrifice." In us it becomes *aware of itself* and calls us into the depths of our humanity. Nichol believes that creation came to its greatest fulfillment (with total awareness and freedom) in Christ Jesus[5] — one among us, the most profound expression, our redeeming fulfillment, what Teilhard calls the "Omega Point" of all of creation.

The Christ vision presented here calls us to our deepest center, to our most authentic interiority and self-possession, even as we "give ourselves away." This means that, for us, "economic and political and technological unions are not sufficient. We must join together precisely as persons,"[6] say *yes* to the "Grand Option" as Bruteau calls it, and out of our most profound freedom give ourselves up. When commenting on Teilhard's thought here, Bruteau takes pains to insist that the functional classifications whose insufficiency we discussed in the previous chapter in relation to our primary faith experience — race, status, achievements, nationality, position, etc. — are not what our evolutionary commitment to unity, to *human community*, ought to focus on. She points out that the very heart of our personhood lies "deeper than these tangential relations and must be able to make you be *you*." It must be able to allow us "to unite ourselves with *all* other persons," not just with those we take a liking to, are emotionally attached to, or even professionally connected to:

If we are to effect the creative union with *all* other persons, we will need to do it from a center in ourselves that is free of the fluctuations of these circumstantial feelings.... This power of self-action in total freedom is precisely what we can all discover to be the most central selfhood in ourselves, the most deeply intimate reality of our being as persons, that which is purely and truly my "I," no matter what my [other] characteristics are. My real "I" is not a bunch of statistics but an existential energy by which I live and act. As my own most intimate energy, it has more warmth and vibrancy than my fluctuating emotions.[7]

There is here then a genuine choice *for* community, a sincere acceptance of the family of creation. The love that Teilhard talks about as the power for community drives us beyond our individualism to unite toward what evolution requests of us. Our *yes* to this love is what he sees as *our* step toward the fulfillment of all things in Christ; for the community we are asked to build will subsume and embrace everything that has gone before, and all of creation will be blessed.

Situating Ourselves

Both Nichol and Teilhard, as I have mentioned, see the example and the fulfillment of this evolutionary next step as having been realized already in the person and vision of Christ Jesus. In a way, then, those of us drawn to this vision ought to experience ourselves as called toward a fullness that is here already, that became conscious in the universe some two thousand years ago, and that now offers us the option, calling forth our acceptance, as it has in fact done through the ages. Christianity, interestingly enough, speaks to Christ's presence among us as "the fullness of time," as "the beginning and the end" — the realization of total "self-gift." In a strange and paradoxical way then, and seen within the linear time of ordinary perception, it would seem that we are called to evolve toward our past — "backward," if you will — toward that which already is in him and awaits our homecoming. Our past, so to speak, is our future. We are called to make real in our lives the vision of authentic humanity already modeled for us and present, one might say, in the collective psyche of our humanity. It is offered over and over again to us, as Christ Jesus — through his living — in fact offered it to those who followed him long ago.

This is an amazing thought, a powerful invitation, not to be taken lightly!

Facing Our Reality

At this point, however, the questions we asked ourselves in chapter 1 need once again to be surfaced. They concern the actuality, the concrete realization of all this in our lives: community, freely embraced in love, is what Teilhard offers as the next evolutionary step, and is what Christ Jesus identified as foundational for his followers. Community is proclaimed as essential by our religion as well and seen as the core meaning of church. "Faith community," "community of believers," "parish community," etc., are the words we use to describe ourselves as church.

I cannot help thinking that the interpretation of these concepts in terms of a "discipleship of equals" (the way scholarship concerned with the earliest Christian movement, that is, community, describes the "realized" vision of Jesus) would have delighted Teilhard de Chardin:

> Sophia, the God of Jesus, wills the wholeness and humanity of everyone and therefore enables the Jesus movement to become a *"discipleship of equals."* They are called to one and the same praxis of *inclusiveness* and *equality* lived by Jesus-Sophia ... to announce to everyone ... God's gracious future, among the impoverished, the starving, the tax-collectors, sinners, and prostitutes.[8]

Jesus had picked his community from among these very ones, had accepted them and loved them into dignity. And, thus, what he offered, and

> what they offered was not an alternative lifestyle but an *alternative ethos:* they were those without a future, but now they had hope again; they were the "outcast" and marginal people in their society, but now they had community again; they were despised and downtrodden, but now they had dignity and self-confidence ... ; they were ... sinners with no hope to share in the holiness and presence of God, but now they were ... experiencing the gracious goodness of

God who had made them equal to the holy and
righteous of Israel.[9]

The ethos described here is hardly easy to live and model.
It was, in many respects, even more difficult in the time
of Jesus than it is today. In his now classic work *Rediscovering the Teaching of Jesus*, Norman Perrin argues that
the radical inclusiveness and sense of community on the
part of Jesus (especially as witnessed in his "table fellowship of the Kingdom of God" and his acceptance of
sinners and outcasts, including "Jews who had made themselves as Gentiles") was most likely the very reason for
his final rejection and betrayal by his own religious leaders and his ultimate crucifixion by the Roman occupying
force.[10] To share the table with outcasts and sinners in
the name of God was unfathomable and deeply offensive to the religious leaders of his time — truly beyond
forgiveness.

In the face of this radical and utterly countercultural
and "dangerous" behavior on the part of Jesus, I cannot
help wondering — in fact the question haunts me — where
has his vision gone? How does Catholicism, in particular,
respond to it today, or perhaps more honestly, why doesn't
it do so? Why does this vision seem so starkly absent from
our religion's official "radar screens"? I mention this here
particularly in the light of contemporary problems tearing
the church apart, but also in the light of church history and
in spite of proclamations about being a "faith community"
made over and over again by our institutional leadership
holding proudly to its apostolic succession.

Why is it that so many of us do not even connect anymore in the day-to-day living out of our religion with Christ's ancient vision of inclusiveness? Why has it become almost commonplace (either accepted or treated with indifference by most of us) to hear church leaders deny table fellowship to gays and lesbians taking a stand on their orientation, to those who want to further stem-cell research, to those who want respect for a woman's right to choose an abortion? It would seem that we understand membership in the church today more like belonging to a club, where living up to prescribed standards, obeying certain rules, accepting precedent, and paying one's dues give one acceptance. Today, to be a Catholic (perhaps more so than the experience of membership in other Christian denominations) does not require much thought, let alone discussion. It does, however, require obedience and acquiescence. There is a crisis in our relationship to the Christian vision. Its energy was certainly there in its inception and, we want to believe, inspired the early church. Culture, however, and the numbing effects of power seem to have had a way of swallowing up those who would call for conversion. A "community of equals" and the loving acceptance of all — even those one disagrees with or perceives as sinners — was perhaps too hard an ideal to follow in a patriarchal age.

Women were clearly its primary, though certainly not the only, victims. They remain victimized even today. "The cultural milieu of early Christianity was a patriarchal and androcentric one — male activity and male humanity were assumed to be normative."[11] The vision of Jesus in its call to inclusiveness and equality, therefore, did not last long—both among the Jews and among the Romans and Hellenes to whom it was proclaimed. As Mary T. Malone observes, the institution of Christianity quickly adopted "the principles of the exclusion of women from public roles and responsibilities, and no words of Jesus seemed to have been heard strongly enough to challenge this."[12]

Sad to say, very little has changed over the centuries. To be sure, we no longer burn creative women as witches, and in the public arena women have gained much ground. Institutional religion with its hierarchical male leadership, however, has hardly been a motivator here, and for the most part has resisted it every step of the way.[13] In Christianity as a whole, "equality" seems to be a rare phenomenon if not a non-concept.

The Burden of the Past

The highpoint of enculturation of the Christian religion into the Greco-Roman worldview came early in the second decade of the fourth century with Christianity's official acceptance by the emperor Constantine. By then, a majority of Christians were Gentiles. The predominantly Greco-Roman order of life and law was theirs, and Greek metaphysics with its emphasis on the unity and permanence of truth ruled their way of understanding themselves, their religion, and the reality of the world they lived in. They had accepted Christianity into their culture and adapted it accordingly. The great diversity, initially characteristic of the Christian religion, had slowly and with great pain and strife been eliminated during the preceding centuries. It had been reduced to the self-proclaimed orthodox[14] version "of Christianity found predominantly, though not exclusively, in the church of Rome."[15]

The persecutions that had raged to eliminate Christianity, particularly from the middle of the third century on, had finally ended by 313 CE when official toleration of Christians was pronounced throughout the empire. With Constantine's acceptance (312 CE) and subsequent patronage, power was given to the leaders of the Christian religion, and quickly the once persecuted church became a persecutor instead. Bart Ehrman summarizes it well:

> Christians were exclusivistic in their views. They believed that the one and only true God had given one way of salvation, and that the only way to be right with this God was through this way he had provided — the death and resurrection of Jesus. This exclusivity . . . bred an intolerance toward religious diversity. Since there was only one way of salvation, all other religions were in error. And being in error carried eternal consequences. Those who did not accept the one true God by believing in the death and resurrection of his Son for salvation would be condemned to the flames of hell for all eternity.[16]

From very early on in Christianity, error had no rights, and Jews and pagans, as well as Christians who did not agree with the orthodox version (heretics), were seen as rejected by God:

> Salvation was dependent on faith.... Faith was *in*
> something; it had content. The content therefore,
> mattered. The *regula fidei* and then the creeds that de-
> veloped were ways to indicate what it was that people
> had to believe. Those who rejected the true beliefs ad-
> hered, necessarily, to false ones. But since only right
> belief can bring salvation, wrong belief can do noth-
> ing but bring damnation. As a result, heretics would
> pay for their false teachings with eternal torment.[17]

This torment, of course, often began here on earth. History has recorded it, and its scars (especially in the form of
guilt and the unwillingness to think freely about religious
issues and to question interpretations) are still felt today.

The scope of our reflection does not permit us to explore how much the logic arguing the "orthodox" view
was motivated by power and the necessary drive to eliminate opposition by all possible means in order to stay in
control. Unity of belief and in interpreting the creedal
mysteries became primary to Christianity-in-power, and
emperors called councils to anathematize diversity, help sta-
bilize belief, and thus, hopefully, bring unity also to their
realm.[18] Needless to say, there did not seem to be much
room or desire for the radical inclusiveness of Jesus. In
many respects, church history, in spite of its holy women
and men, is a tale of abuse of power and of shame. The
secular support for "Christendom" by various types of gov-
ernments has, of course, largely disappeared today. What
frightens me in reflecting on our past, however, is the realization of how very close we are today, once again or

perhaps still, to the logic, philosophy, and rationalizations of control.

Structures of Domination

With power officially bestowed upon it, the Christian church of the Hellenic world also quite naturally adopted the organizational and structural elements of the society in which it found itself. Bishops became princes and started to behave like princes. Popes became monarchs and extended their secular power, as time moved on and the opportunity presented itself. As political structures changed, adaptations were made. Papal control either expanded through wars or excommunications, or it declined — when emperors, kings, and ultimately dictators rebelled. Leadership, in style and practice, however, largely remained "domination" and never adequately returned to the pastoral dimension it was meant for. Even to this day, and in spite of the considerable reform attempts by the Second Vatican Council, the structures of the church can be recognized as vestiges of feudal/mediaeval times.

The feudal system was based on land, loyalty, and the need for security. It was hierarchical in nature, with the king or emperor on the highest rung bestowing land to overlords in return for their sworn loyalty. They, in turn, had their vassals, who provided military service to them and in return were granted land, worked by serfs — usually powerless, uneducated, and voiceless.[19] "The entire system was grounded on a rock-hard foundation — in promised *loyalty,* in fact, homage to one's feudal master or superior,"

Donald Cozzens writes. "In all feudal systems, loyalty and accountability were always *upward:* vassals never report to serfs, lords of the manor are never accountable to their vassals. And dialogue, especially dialogue involving serfs, was quite literally unthinkable."[20]

It should not be surprising to anyone raised in the Roman Catholic religion (with its direct and uninterrupted lineage to antiquity and the subsequent feudal system) to recognize clear parallels in our ecclesial structure and conduct even to this day. The silencing process of theologians whose thoughts are not considered "loyal" to the ruling curia[21] is a case in point. This is particularly true for those theologians belonging to a religious congregation and, therefore, bound by vow to obey. In their case, curial communication, let alone dialogue, is rarely if ever directly with the writer. He or she may be asked to respond to questions in writing, but the curial judgment is handed down to the major superior whose loyal obedience in carrying out the curial decree — silencing or even dismissing "the subject" — is expected.

Perhaps no one has described the mediaeval power structure of the church with greater integrity and honesty than has Donald Cozzens (himself a priest of the diocese of Cleveland) in his book *Faith That Dares to Speak:*

> The pope — the sovereign or king in our parallel structure — grants benefices (i.e., dioceses) to his bishops. The bishops in turn promise obedience, homage, and loyalty to their sovereign, the bishop of Rome.... The bishops, in turn, grant benefices (i.e.,

parishes) to their priests, who promise obedience, homage, and loyalty to the chief shepherd of their diocese. At least from the middle of the nineteenth century in the U.S., parishes were run like fiefdoms. And it is not unusual, even in our post–Vatican II church, to find pastors who still perceive their parish as a benefice or a fiefdom. Even more sobering, some pastors continue to look upon parishioners as more or less uneducated sheep.[22]

They were, furthermore, encouraged to do so in their priestly training — learning that there was a stark difference between themselves, *in persona Christi,* and the ordinary "folks in the pew." Pope Pius X was, perhaps, the most honest about all of this: he saw the church as inherently unequal and uses the "pastor and flock" analogy to make his point unambiguously. Cozzens cites from *Vehementer Nos:* "So distinct are these categories [of pastor and flock] that with the pastoral body only rests the necessary right and authority for promoting the end of the society [the church] and directing all its members toward that end." As Pius X sees it, "The only duty of the multitude is to allow themselves to be led, and, like a docile flock, to follow the pastor."[23] In this way, their salvation is secure. Whether in matters of parish or diocesan protocol, of moral behavior, or of doctrinal or scriptural interpretation, Father was seen to have the answer. And the subservient question, "Do we *have* to believe this?" became the standard Catholic way of handling it all.

Why is it that so many of us do not even connect anymore in the day-to-day living out of our religion with Christ's ancient vision of inclusiveness?

In our time, the expected subservience of parishioners in the Roman Catholic institution is perhaps no more clearly demonstrated than when they are forbidden to hold meetings in the church they have built with their own money by pastors — acting often out of loyalty to their bishops — who disagree with the purpose of the meeting. Concerned Catholics, for example, who question episcopal behavior with respect to the sexual scandals in their diocese are considered disloyal when they organize in order to ask for accountability from their leaders. We know what Jesus had to say about scandal to little ones (Mark 9:42), but then Jesus would probably not recognize the power structure that now claims him as its head.

Jesus also had much to say about pointing the finger at others while denying one's own culpability, and here again the feudal structure (with upward, not downward, accountability) opens the way to major abuse. The recent episcopal decree (intended, no doubt, to signal concern about pedophilia among the clergy) that virtually denies entrance into the seminary to homosexual applicants — demanding, among other things, proof of previous sexual abstinence not demanded from anyone else — not only ignores the existing reality of diverse sexual orientations present in the priesthood and episcopate, but also unjustly attempts to blame an already oppressed minority in this culture for behavior not in any way related to their orientation. One cannot help wondering whether such rulings are motivated by the desire to defuse the embarrassing attention given to the truly blameworthy behavior on the part of bishops and diocesan staff in the past that furthered sexual abuse by ignoring it and simply moving pedophiles and other sex offenders from parish to parish in order to avoid facing the problem.

Loyalty to the system is so deeply embedded in the Catholic psyche that it is unquestioningly given primacy. The one who questions abuse or other inappropriate behavior is labeled the abuser instead. Concerned parishioners are seen "to have trouble with legitimate authority." They are, therefore, declared radical, or angry, or aggressive, as having no respect and only "thinking of themselves" rather than the common good.

From Religion Back to Faith

But of what use is a structure in our time that models a culture no longer in existence? Of what use is a religion that approaches the divine with unerring certainty, that holds dogma as unchanging and rejects the discoveries of its time with unblinking arrogance when they are contrary or perhaps merely inconvenient to the long outmoded creedal formulae that control its members? Of what use is a religion, for that matter, that rejects change in a world where there is nothing permanent *except* change? Of what good is an institution that is threatened by innovation and creativity in its members, that rejects thinking which ventures beyond ancient categories, and acts as if accepted scientific data do not exist?

As I have indicated, my attempts to draw some distinctions between primordial faith, spirituality, and religion in the previous chapter were motivated by the hope to open up the possibility for explorations beyond the strictures both in religious interpretation and institutional structure discussed above. I did this not out of disrespect for the religion I love, but out of fear for its relevance. My sense is that the Christian religions as a whole, but Catholicism in particular, are in dire need of primordial faith energy and the wonder with which it gifts us. For many of us, having our behavior regulated and answers given to us — often before we ask or are even interested — simply no longer works, especially if the answers no longer speak to the questions, or may not even have questions that require them.

The very concept of having answers "provided" speaks against the questing that we recognize today as essential to the mature faith journey. My intention in the last two chapters has been to give the phenomenon of "religion" some boundaries in order to distinguish it from the institution that houses it but should not be identified with it. I suggested a somewhat different task for spirituality and primordial faith consisting of the former's initial symbolic and ritual expression of the latter's human questing into, and subsequent depth *yes* to, the Mystery. My hope in this was to provide "space" beyond ancient and often archaic strictures, and to allow individual believers (Christians and, specifically, Catholics) the room for movement and the opportunity for finding their place on the journey into the Holy that their life is meant to be. The rest of this book will venture into the terrain opened up for us this way and explore what I hope are relevant themes of

Christianity. We will want to do this with respect for our heritage as well as for the present world perspective.

Thoughts and Questions for Meditation

What are your thoughts concerning the following selections from chapter 3?

1. For Teilhard, creation is progression, with ever greater interiority and self-possession, toward "community." It comes about through a process of self-gift toward union and for the sake of greater consciousness. The movement is at first brought about simply by the evolutionary intent itself until eventually, in us, human consciousness allows for recognition, and our self-awareness and freedom invite us to enter this process and say *yes* to its integrity. In this way, the possibility opens up for us to become "the uniting elements" that further evolution and upon whom it depends.

2. Teilhard identifies as *love* the creative energy that we hold in common — the *human* energy that calls us toward union. It is this most intimate energy of ours that we are asked to commit to the new union. . . . The power for community drives us beyond our individualism to unite toward what evolution requests of us. Our *yes* to this love is what Teilhard sees as our step toward the fulfillment of all things in Christ.

3. We are called to make real in our lives the vision of authentic humanity already modeled for us and

present, one might say, in the collective psyche of our humanity.

4. Community is proclaimed as essential by our religion as well and seen as the core meaning of church. "Faith Community," "community of believers," "parish community," etc., are the words we use to describe ourselves as church. Referring back to "Facing Our Reality," and the discussion of Jesus' inclusive table fellowship, can you identify with this concept of community as your reality of church?

5. What is your reaction to the section "Structures of Domination"?

6. Of what use is a structure in our time that models a culture no longer in existence? Of what use is a religion that approaches the divine with unerring certainty, that holds dogma as unchanging and rejects the discoveries of its time with unblinking arrogance when they are contrary or perhaps merely inconvenient to the long outmoded creedal formulae that control its members? Of what use is a religion, for that matter, that rejects change in a world where there is nothing permanent *except* change? Of what good is an institution that is threatened by innovation and creativity in its members, that rejects thinking which ventures beyond ancient categories, and acts as if accepted scientific data do not exist?

7. My sense is that the Christian religions as a whole, but Catholicism in particular, are in dire need of primordial faith energy and the wonder with which it gifts us.

For many of us, having our behavior regulated and answers given to us — often before we ask or are even interested — simply no longer works, especially if the answers no longer speak to the questions, or may not even have questions that require them.

❦ FOUR ❦

Expanding Our Horizons

Where were you when I laid the foundations of the earth?
Tell me, if you have understanding.
Have you commanded the morning since your days
*   began?*
Have you entered into the springs of the sea,
or walked in the recesses of the deep?
Do you know the ordinances of the heavens?
Can you establish their rule on the earth?

—Job 38:4, 12, 16, 33

On Seeing with New Eyes

At the beginning of her book *A New Set of Eyes*, Paula D'Arcy tells a revealing story about an experience in the early seventies when she, and two hundred other counselors and educators attending a workshop at Yale University, were invited to solve (without pen or paper) a word problem with a mathematical answer. The organizers wanted the groups that formed around three different answers to convince each other of the correctness of their solution and left them in the Yale auditorium to work it out. It was, as the group discovered — but not immediately, nor easily — an exercise in group dynamics and peer pressure. The initial calculations had yielded a large group whose answer was 38, a smaller but substantial group whose answer was 21, and two men who believed the answer to be 11. When the organizers returned, the largest group had become a clear majority. The second group now numbered only 35 persons. The two men who believed the answer to be 11 had not convinced anyone else, but also had not changed their minds.

"I remember the evening with a certain vividness," D'Arcy writes. "The correct answer was revealed to be 11. For myself, I had never entertained that possibility, clearly and logically having concluded that two individuals could not accurately see what one hundred and ninety-eight did not."[1] Why, after all, would anyone not agree with the majority solution, or even, the collective hunch?

It seems that for many of us our understanding of truth has somehow become "democratized": There is the notion that if the majority believes something, it must be so. "Many beliefs (especially religious beliefs) are so widely established," observes D'Arcy, "that it appears 'unthinkable' to question them." Even a quiet "wondering" whether they make sense anymore, whether one can speak them without reserve — as in the creed, for example — threatens us with alienation from the group.[2]

It is true, of course, that Christianity, and certainly the Catholic religion in its official interpretation of dogma, hardly claims "majority rule." It prefers, instead, to take the path of "divine revelation." The effects of stifling independent thought and questioning, nevertheless, are the same, since the majority accepts magisterial proclamations and expects them to be correct. A certain "group think" is encouraged this way. There is real angst, it seems, that causes us to shrink from any serious "thinking-through," or possible reconsideration, of the "articles of faith" and what they might mean for us today.

The history of this angst, as was discussed in the previous chapter, unfortunately dates into antiquity and is therefore well established. From early on in its "orthodox" period the church met doubt and disagreement with "holy" polemic, and Catholics even up to the Second Vatican Council were brought up to see such disagreement as a sin. To this very day "thinking for oneself," especially if it opens up to questions that could threaten magisterial opinion, is not encouraged in Catholic seminaries and theology schools. Professors take oaths of allegiance, papal letters forbid discussion of controversial subjects, and, as was mentioned earlier, scholars who suggest alternative ways of seeing long and "universally" held interpretations of religious and moral topics are still silenced or have their academic faculties removed.

D'Arcy applies her Yale experience to her own deeply personal faith quest, however, and to the personal maturity it requires. She observes correctly that it is "so much easier to embrace religion than it is to encounter God." There is no comfort zone, no infallible way, no predesigned model for meeting God. "I can find no reassuring doctrine that predicts exactly what steps to take, and how things will unfold," D'Arcy observes. "There is only a growing awareness that the lens through which I view my life is small;

that my cherished views are perhaps only echoes of what
is true."[3]

The Struggle of Job

What perhaps may be of help to those of us whose struggles are similar to those expressed so well in D'Arcy's
little book is the assurance that human response to reality — all of it, no matter how obvious or mysterious —
is always expressed within the context of the culture and
time in which it takes place. It is limited, for better or
worse, to the knowledge framework of *that* culture and
that time. Enculturation, therefore, is ever a part of the
written and spoken word in any religion and, as we have
discussed, Christianity's views of and about God are no
exception.

That, in a sense, is what the book of Job is really about:
He had to let go of his culture's ancient and "sacralized"
experience of God — a God who rewarded the just, pun-
ished the wicked and, therefore, should not have "allowed"
Job to suffer so. This view had been "absolutized" in Job's
time. He and his friends and his family had come to expect
their lives to be ordered by it, and so he was put through
torturous questioning by his friends to discover what evil
he had done. The citation placed at the beginning of this
chapter is intended to have us face the Job within each one
of us, to prepare us, in other words, for the major reversals
in our religious theories and expectations that are surfacing
today.[4]

All of us without exception have only limited vision in every aspect of our lives, for mystery pervades all of reality and ever has us encounter our poverty. What then can any finite being, what can even (and I observe this with the utmost respect) a papal finite being *know* about God? Revelation, even at its most profound, is always *to* humans *as* humans and will, therefore, always be subject to interpretation within the human context (language, culture, gender, age, geography, cosmology, philosophy, politics, need for power, etc.) in which it occurs.[5]

An Example for Today

The ascension of Jesus into heaven, for example, or the assumption of his mother, need to be understood as first having been visualized within a context that experienced a totally different cosmology than we know today. Heaven, and God who dwelled there, was thought to be "above." Jesus, thus, went up and disappeared into the clouds to sit at God's right hand.

The ancient understanding of the universe that would allow for this way of "seeing" has, indeed, a very revered past. Its origins date back to paleolithic times,[6] when the sky was experienced as a powerful and mysterious dome. From it came light and rain, thunder and lightning. It stood for numinous power beyond human comprehension or control. "When people aspired towards the transcendence represented by the sky, they felt that they could escape from the frailty of the human condition and pass to what lies beyond," explains Karen Armstrong.[7] They also encountered its mysterious and life-threatening forces. It filled them with awe and often with fear, even as it gave them a sense of dependence and hope.

Today, however, we know that there really is no "up" or "down" in the universe. We do not live on a plate but on a revolving globe whose up or down is relative to where one lives. What is "up" for us is "down" for people living on the other side of the globe, and vice versa. What is "above us" is the universe of which, amazingly, each of us is also the center. What is "below" is the universe as well. Einstein, much to his dismay, discovered that the universe is indeed expanding in all directions and does so from every point in the universe. For a long time, and understandably, he was very uncomfortable with this revolutionary and very foreign discovery. He tried for years to hide it from the world in order to allow what had "worked" for so long to continue. This obfuscation was, by his own admission, one of his greatest blunders.[8] For him too "reconsidering strong and cherished beliefs [was] a formidable step."[9] Paula D'Arcy observes thoughtfully: "Perhaps this is why we seldom question the largest things, or why Galileo was imprisoned."[10]

The Power of Symbol and Metaphor

By offering these considerations, I do not imply, of course, that the doctrines of the ascension and of the assumption need to be eliminated. What I do suggest is that their symbolic/metaphoric nature needs to be taken seriously; that it needs to be allowed to move us beyond the literal, and what is perceived as "factual," into greater depth. It is of little use to insist that there is a place "up there" where Jesus went and where all of us will go if we believe. Once we know what we know, a different approach is mandated or religion becomes irrelevant and even silly.

Treating the truths of our religion as primarily historical and factual deprives us of their deeper meaning and creates unnecessary problems often causing unwarranted harm. We run the danger of having ever unfolding discoveries in the various sciences continuously point out the flaws of what we claim to be the "facts of revelation" — "facts," which science once held as certain but now understands differently; "facts," which we used for our interpretation and are now forced to rethink if we want to retain credibility.

Still greater harm caused by "factualism" in religion is, however, the destruction of, or total disregard for, numinosity itself. The Holy "breaks into" the human condition brought to the limits of its own knowing and power. It can never be contained nor controlled there, however, and any attempt to do so reduces the religious enterprise to mere posturing and empty words. Job learned this after great suffering — the destruction of his entire world. It is my fear that in today's religious climate we may be forced to learn it that way as well, unless we allow ourselves to be moved to depth faith, once again, and to be taught there by Mystery itself. "Belonging to God feels without precedent," says Paula D'Arcy. "If I alter my sight and follow God, not an image, *I will be changed.*"[11]

In a previous book (*In the Stillness You Will Know*) while discussing metaphor in religious language, I described it as the speaking about God that allows finitude to approach infinite Mystery, a speaking "that acknowledges its own inadequacy while recognizing, at the same time, our need for communication." It is a speaking, I said, that allows for the realization that everything uttered about God is "true" as well as "not true," contains an "is" and also an "is not," a "yes" and a "no." I suggested that "all authentic language about God, all naming, and all helpful images of the Mystery that is God are of necessity analogical."[12] This insight is, of course, in no way new. Thomas said as much in the Middle Ages, but religion, it would seem, has had a tendency to forget it and to objectify God language instead.

Metaphor is a way of speaking that creatively sustains the tension between the "yes" and the "no," the "is" and the "is not," which arises whenever we honestly and humbly approach Mystery. As such, it helps us move into the symbolic and to avoid literalism; to admit our poverty, our lack, in the face of the overwhelming and "wholly other" — that which, in the words of Rudolf Otto, is "beyond the sphere of the usual, the intelligible, and the familiar, which therefore falls quite outside the limits of [what we can know], . . . filling the mind with blank wonder and astonishment."[13]

"Factualism," on the other hand, is oblivious of the profoundly symbolic nature of God language. Because of the discomfort experienced in the face of the "wholly other," it moves into denial in the form of literalism, absolutizes the "is" and ignores the "is not." In so doing, it resorts to what it knows best: rationalizations which, Otto suggests, end up "constructing such a massive structure of theory and such a plausible fabric of interpretation, that the 'mystery' is frankly excluded.... The fundamental fact of religious experience," what I have called primary faith, "is, as it were, simply rolled out so thin and flat as to be finally eliminated altogether."[14] This is the danger of all fundamentalism and also, I believe, of some Catholic dogmatism. Literalism (even in the face of overwhelming evidence that it can no longer be meaningfully sustained) takes the depth out of the faith experience and "flattens" it.

The cosmos of fundamentalist Christianity to which I referred above is a case in point. If the risen Christ ascended, that is, went upward into heaven, then heaven is quite literally a place — up there somewhere, to be attained after death by all those who are saved. Hell is another "place," as well, in the opposite direction. God too is seen as out and up there, and our God imagery becomes one of separation and distance. I suppose we ourselves are situated somewhere in the middle between "up there" and "down there." We raise our hearts and look up when we pray, and somehow we expect the God "up there" to be watching us, answering our prayers and communicating God's wishes.

In line with this religious "geography," we also expect God to have "made" this place for us and situated it where it is (some think in six days — like the work week some live by). Like everything else, God has "made" us as well. This divine craftsman who made us is, of course, also the one who will take our life away when he (and a "he" it is — the entire patriarchal culture still extant will insist on that) sees fit. In this literalist model, we really do not see ourselves as having very much to do, except to accept and endure it. That is why, when we are aware of death, we implore God to give us a bit more time or to hasten our going.

The view described here has its origin for the most part in the Middle Ages and in Greco-Roman antiquity before that. It proposes a world neatly divided into realms of spirit and matter, with the former to be worked toward and the latter to be avoided as much as possible. It knew nothing of an evolving universe, of our bodies as mammalian and as expressions of this evolving universe. For it, the cosmos was a material construct that could easily be deconstructed by the divine maker. We were created with a rational soul — in God's image (one reason why we find it relatively easy to "make" God in *our* image as well). Being thus created, we were destined to control the rest of creation, which is inferior to us — non-rational, and, therefore, dependent on us.

But what would our faith life be like if we took the sacred stories of religion and brought them into the worldview of our day, into an understanding of the cosmos that is radically different — not because of some whimsical opinion poll but because of the discoveries of science? What would it be like if we moved beyond the kind of schizophrenic attitude that accepts science and its marvels in our day-to-day thinking, but ignores its discoveries and wonder when it gets to prayer and to our God contact? What if, in other words, we accepted the universe — as it is emerging in our day — into our religious self-reflection?

There is today no reason anymore to think in separatist terms. Not only is there no "up" or "down" in the universe in which we find ourselves, there is, in fact, no "in" or "out," no separation of anything from anything, anywhere and at any time. The image for the universe today comes closer to that of an organism than that of a mechanism — with independent or disconnected parts in space and time that can simply be destroyed without affecting anything else. In an organism everything is connected to, affecting, and affected by everything else, and there is constant change for the sake of life and the new.

The interconnectedness of our cosmos is clarified perhaps even more by the holographic perspective offered by contemporary physics. It sees the universe as a hologram, each part of which contains the whole, and is, therefore, intimately involved with it, and affected by it and every other part.[15] In the world of today "all things and all moments touch each other at every point."[16] I wrote elsewhere that

> a physics that discovers reality as interlaced and interwoven, that discovers the presence of the whole in each part and each part connected to every other part, that sees mind and matter as, in fact, inextricably linked with each part of the universe, containing, in some sense, the entire universe, challenges a metaphysics of exclusion and [separation] to its very core by the utter and uncompromising relationality which it presents as foundational to all of reality. The implications of this are staggering, for as the science that was normative for so much of our modern worldview literally implodes, the theology built on its dicta

needs to re-examine its perspectives as well or become irrelevant and obsolete with it.[17]

Experiencing the Holy

Where then is God, and how can one experience the Holy? A little vignette comes to mind that in its simplicity says it all: A little fish keeps asking its mother: "Mommy, Mommy, when will we get to the water"? The mother finally turns to it and says gently: "Honey, you are in it. It is all around you. Without it you could not swim. It sustains your very life."

The universe we are contemplating today presents the possibility of seeing God just like that water: "O God, where are you"? cries the suffering soul. And the answer comes from deep in the cosmos — the center of which is in each one of us: "Honey, I am in you and all around you. I am the energy that flows through you and sustains you. In me you live and move and have your being. You do not have to 'come home.' *You already are*." Our embodied way of being is not always capable of grasping the full reality of this,[18] and it is perhaps better to let it seep into us slowly and through contemplation. Things start looking different when we do this. Death, for example, no longer is seen as an "end" so much, but rather as a "movement" toward awareness, toward a deeper level — unimpeded by physical barriers. The latter, of course, had their place and were important for our sojourn here on earth, but in death they yield the light, if you will, which they can no longer contain.

What would our faith life be like if we took the sacred stories of religion and brought them into the worldview of our day, into an understanding of the cosmos that is radically different — not because of some whimsical opinion poll but because of the discoveries of science?

"She has passed," not "passed *on*" so much as passed *into* another way of experiencing, into another modality of being that is no longer in need of the body. "Passed *beyond* the veil" would perhaps be a more accurate description of death for the reality in which we find ourselves today, since there is, in fact, no "elsewhere," no "other place." Science calls this "non-locality," pointing to the *here* of interconnectivity and the *now* that holds within it the past and extends its energy throughout the cosmos.

Perhaps Jodie Foster's experience as a scientist in the movie *Contact* comes closest in meaning to the "passing" I am inviting us to reflect on, though hers is not an experience of actual death. In the movie, she has the sense of traveling through time and space with enormous speed in a spacecraft designed for this purpose. After the experience, she discovers, however, that what she has seen and learned happened to her in what might be called "no time" at all, and "nowhere else" but on this very planet earth — clearly out of a different mode of perception (on a different "frequency") where time and space implode.

The God of the universe we are contemplating today is clearly not a God "outside" us, controlling from another place, from the outside in. The ocean for which the little fish was searching does not control the fish. It holds it and sustains it. So too, our God holds us. God is *in* the event that *we are*, not outside it. Asking questions, therefore, such as, "Why did God permit this to happen?" or making statements about God "wanting" a primarily "chocolate" population for the rebuilt city of New Orleans, about God punishing Ariel Sharon with a stroke for dividing the Holy

Land, simply no longer fit. They belong to a potentate who operates externally. The universe, if you will, is not "manipulated" by God. God does not win wars for us. God does not "let us down" when we lose them either. God does not send us tornadoes or tsunamis or earthquakes.

The God of the emerging worldview can, I believe, be found primarily *in* creation, working *through* creation (and, in that sense, through us in whom creation comes to consciousness and freedom), not *against* it. The universe, and everything that comprises the universe, is unfolding, changing, and evolving. And we are part of all of it *as we are* — finite organisms with life and love energy that passes through us and at some moment moves on — when the organisms can no longer hold our fire. This is how, I suggest, we might understand death: as the surrendering of the fire. "Life is changed," in death, "not taken away." We do not end; we simply change into another mode of being where we continue to grow into God — into the infinite Light and Love — ever present also in the here and the now.

What I offer, then, for a contemporary faith understanding of "life hereafter" is that (knowing what we do of the universe today) it makes little sense to talk of a "going away" to another place. "Heaven" is here. It is what the universe is — a dynamic situation, where transformation and divinization continues. Dying is painful only because the light that we are needs to leave the body. The separation can be painful both for us and for those who are not as yet ready to experience the form of being we are being called to. The fear of the unknown — that which we do not yet see or understand — can be painful (much like in birth). But death is neither the end of us, nor really the end of our care for those we love.

Julian of Norwich had the right message for our time: "All shall be well; all manner of things shall be well."

Paul was right also, when he suggested that now "we only see through a glass darkly" (1 Cor. 13:12).

My mother was right, when in a dream (perhaps more correctly out of "dream time" as the Australian Aborigines would say) her message to me was, "Do not fret over the sad way in which I died; for, my little girl, right now you see only as out of a peep hole."

The Power of the Ascension

The universe to which we belong is one of perpetual transformation. Our realizing this restores long-lost dignity to the reality of change. The worldview of our time treasures interconnectedness with everyone and everything and moves us away from the illusion of individualism, separation, superiority, and inferiority. We belong to a cosmic family, and the link of our interconnectedness is Love, eternal and powerful Love. For Christians this Love reached the fullness of expression in Jesus of Nazareth, a human being who in the fullness of who he was showed us our destiny. We dwell in his energy. We were baptized into it, walked into its waters. If only we could accept it and embrace its power.

And it is here that we want to reconnect with our reflection on the ascension of Jesus, and Mary's assumption. The

worldview that is emerging in our time, as we have seen, no
longer relates to the spatial categories of the past that are
insisted upon still by what I have called the "factualism" of
fundamentalists. "Absorption into the energy field that is
God," then, or "fusion with the divine" are possible ways in
which I try to understand these dogmas. The *Catechism of
the Catholic Church* actually suggests this. About the ascension of Jesus it observes, "Jesus' final apparition ends with
the irreversible entry of his humanity into divine glory."
It references the metaphoric by stating that this event was
"symbolized by the cloud and by heaven, where he is seated
from that time forward at God's right hand."[19] Concerning
Mary's assumption into heaven, the *Catechism* sees it as "a
singular participation in her Son's resurrection and an an-
ticipation of the resurrection of other Christians."[20] Along
with the Declaration on Religious Freedom of the Second
Vatican Council and its Declaration on the Relationship
of the Church to Non-Christian Religions, as well as the
thinking of Teilhard de Chardin and the ultimate convergence of all of creation into the Omega Point which is
Christ, I would want to see Mary's assumption as antici-
pating not just Christians' but all of humanity's ultimate
homecoming into the heart of God.

The symbolism of "being taken up beyond the clouds"
connects us well with the numinous that the sky has represented from of old. It gives us a symbol, a metaphor,
for a sacred moment of divinization, a moment that is our
future also, a moment that awaits our recognition and our
acceptance. We will reflect on this again in the succeeding
chapters.

Thoughts and Questions for Meditation

What are your thoughts concerning the following selections from chapter 4?

1. It seems that for many of us our understanding of truth has somehow become "democratized": there is the notion that if the majority believes something, it must be so. "Many beliefs (especially religious beliefs) are so widely established," observes D'Arcy, "that it appears 'unthinkable' to question them." Even a quiet "wondering" whether they make sense anymore, whether one can speak them without reserve — as in the creed, for example — threatens us with alienation from the group.

2. It is "so much easier to embrace religion than it is to encounter God." There is no comfort zone, no infallible way, no predesigned model for meeting God. "I can find no reassuring doctrine that predicts exactly what steps to take, and how things will unfold," D'Arcy observes. "There is only a growing awareness that the lens through which I view my life is small; that my cherished views are perhaps only echoes of what is true."

3. What perhaps may be of help to those of us whose struggles are similar to those expressed so well in D'Arcy's little book is the assurance that human response to reality — all of it, no matter how obvious or mysterious — is always expressed within the context

of the culture and time in which it takes place. It is limited, for better or worse, to the knowledge framework of *that* culture and *that* time. Enculturation, therefore, is ever a part of the written and spoken word in any religion and, as we have discussed, Christianity's views of and about God are no exception.

4. Revelation, even at its most profound, is always *to* humans *as* humans and will, therefore, always be subject to interpretation within the human context (language, culture, gender, age, geography, cosmology, philosophy, politics, need for power, etc.) in which it occurs.

5. Treating the truths of our religion as primarily historical and factual deprives us of their deeper meaning and creates unnecessary problems often causing unwarranted harm. We run the danger of having ever unfolding discoveries in the various sciences continuously point out the flaws of what we claim to be the "facts of revelation" — "facts," which science once held as certain but now understands differently; "facts," which we used for our interpretation and are now forced to rethink if we want to retain credibility.

6. Still greater harm caused by "factualism" in religion is, however, the destruction of, or total disregard for, numinosity itself. The Holy "breaks into" the human condition brought to the limits of its own knowing and power. It can never be contained nor controlled there, however, and any attempt to do so reduces

the religious enterprise to mere posturing and empty words.

7. What is your reaction to the discussion regarding the ascension of Jesus and the assumption of Mary — inviting a move from literalism to metaphor and a depth appropriation of these insights of our faith?

8. What would our faith life be like if we took the sacred stories of religion and brought them into the worldview of our day, into an understanding of the cosmos that is radically different — not because of some whimsical opinion poll but because of the discoveries of science? What would it be like if we moved beyond the kind of schizophrenic attitude that accepts science and its marvels in our day-to-day thinking, but ignores its discoveries and wonder when it gets to prayer and to our God contact? What if, in other words, we accepted the universe, as it is emerging in our day, into our religious self-reflection?

9. The universe we are contemplating today presents the possibility of seeing God just like the ocean is to the little fish: "O God, where are you"? cries the suffering soul. And the answer comes from deep in the cosmos — the center of which is in each one of us: "Honey, I am in you and all around you. I am the energy that flows through you and sustains you. In me you live and move and have your being. You do not have to 'come home.' *You already are.*"

10. What are your thoughts on death, in the light of your reflections on this chapter?

11. The universe to which we belong is one of perpetual transformation. Our realizing this restores long-lost dignity to the reality of change. The worldview of our time treasures interconnectedness with everyone and everything and moves us away from the illusion of individualism, separation, superiority, and inferiority. We belong to a cosmic family, and the link of our interconnectedness is Love, eternal and powerful Love.

❦ FIVE ❦

An Invitation to Wonder

We are now being called upon to see new things. What this requires is a transformation of self, and the creation of organs of perception, which allow us to see those things.

— Arthur Zajonc

Focusing the Issue

In an interview conducted by Jane Clark with the physicist Arthur Zajonc, he describes the moment of scientific discovery or insight that happens to the creative mind, as epiphanal and deeply mysterious.[1] Its origin, in spite of years of practice and discipline, is ever experienced as beyond one's control or even understanding. "I suppose I think of science as being, in some ways, a spiritual practice," Zajonc observes. It takes discipline to be creative. It takes willingness to change, to look at things differently, to be open to what at first may appear strange or out of the ordinary, to accept the new. "Just as the artist, or the spiritual contemplative, are working not only on outer phenomena, but also working on themselves, so every scientist who makes a discovery has succeeded in creating a new organ of perception."[2]

Zajonc uses Isaac Newton's discovery of the law of gravity as an example of just such an epiphany. It happened during what Newton called his *anni mirabiles* (miraculous years), his years of contemplation, when on the very simple occasion of sitting under an apple tree, he saw an apple fall to the ground and recognized — *saw* in this fall — "the same thing as the moon going overhead." Zajonc, in telling the story, stresses Newton's *seeing,* a perception that was the result of contemplation and years of profound engagement with reality. It had opened him up to the gift of sight and its treasures, which he was subsequently compelled to share with the world.

Watching an apple fall to the ground is certainly not an extraordinary occurrence, and many have "seen" such a simple phenomenon throughout history. Seeing what Newton *saw*, however, was an epiphany. It "changed" the world and how we live in it. Through similar epiphanies of the last century, shared with us by courageous men and women of contemplative vision, we are today being invited, according to Zajonc, into a transformation that requires of us a new set of inner and outer eyes as well. We need these to help us transcend what he calls "cultural determinants which bias us toward seeing the world in certain ways." We are being called to *see* new things.[3]

For many of the scientists, the insights that formed the foundation for the emerging worldview of today were by no means a peaceful experience. They were in fact truly upsetting. These researchers, after all, were tried and true Newtonians, but now they "were creating forms for which there was no previous history. They saw the necessity to develop new ways of thinking which were shocking relative to the ways they were habituated to seeing."[4] It took many of them years to come to grips with this extraordinary turning point — crisis — in their entire way of responding to reality.

"Today our society as a whole finds itself in a similar crisis," observes Fritjof Capra. We are being "shocked" out of the ways we have been used to understanding the world, ways we have used to "see," ways we have taken for granted and felt at home in. It would seem that the scientific discoveries, dating from the beginning of the twentieth century, have finally taken hold of, and are beginning to affect, all other disciplines, as well as the culture dependent on them. Capra wrote his book *The Turning Point: Science, Society and the Rising Culture* a number of years ago to discuss this crisis and its effects in various areas: medicine, economics, psychology, to mention but a few.[5] Religion, though discussed in relation to other topics, is not addressed in its own right in his book. It is, however, the concern of these pages — specifically as the crisis of our time relates to the worldview of traditional Christianity.

Clearly there are a number of ways to help prepare us for necessary re-visioning; for movement toward reappropriating the charter events of our religion and regaining a sense of wonder and of depth faith so easily lost through "factualism" and the excessive logic and intellectualism of the past. My hope in this chapter is to do so by means of reflecting on stories — true events that have occurred during the last several years and that I happened upon almost synchronistically. They were, in a way, moments of epiphany for me and have enabled me to *see* with new eyes. They have led me to take seriously the convergence of disciplines that invites a change in perspective. They also have helped me not to be afraid of paradox in my life, but to come to expect it and to accept it as a given in the world of reality. They have encouraged me, therefore, to accept what is often referred to as the "paranormal" and to begin to see it as perhaps normal instead — as a way of stretching us beyond the narrow confines of our here and now, a way of giving us a deeper realization of the still dormant powers within many of us.

I present these stories here with the hope that they might form a collage, if you will, for our contemplation and subsequent vision transformation. There is clearly some risk involved in doing this, as the stories will seem "out of the ordinary," and readers may wonder what they are doing in a book like this. Perhaps the answer will come if we let the stories simmer a bit in our imagination and allow our intuition some room to play and challenge. We might discover, then, that they are not so strange after all and are simply readying us for capacities already within us but unrecognized and, now, gently awakening and calling us deeper.

Clearly, for me the haunting question ever concerns the consequences that the new worldview will have for religion and religious interpretation. The stories and events shared here will, I hope, enhance wonder and gratitude — essential dispositions, if we are to embrace what is unfolding for us today. In the final chapter we will hopefully be ready, then, to reflect further, more directly and freely, on the transformation of vision that invites itself into our religious tradition.

Transcending Space and Time

I

In April of 1999 a Benedictine sister friend of mine living in California had a powerful dream. She was met in the dream by a dear friend of hers whom she had nursed in his last weeks of struggle with a brain tumor. They had communicated deeply during his time of suffering and committed themselves to "stay connected" once he had "passed over." That night he came to her, embraced her with his energy, and then asked her to go down a pathway leading deep into the ground. On the path she encountered four teenagers. The children seemed very disturbed and upset. They looked to her for help in finding their way. She embraced them with the energy she had received from her friend and showed them the way. With that the dream ended.

My friend saw it as a strong dream but could not make out what its meaning for her was. Two weeks later she found out when she saw the pictures of the four youngsters on the front page of the newspaper. They were four of the teenagers that had been killed by their schoolmates in Littleton, Colorado.

II

Another story — quite different, but also challenging our linear conception of time, happened to a missionary doctor in the Congo.

She had worked hard to help a mother in the labor ward of a tiny clinic but, in spite of everything she had done, she could not save the mother's life, though she was able to deliver her tiny premature baby daughter. There was no incubator in the clinic to keep the baby alive, however, nor were there any special feeding facilities. To help as much as possible in what seemed to be a hopeless situation, a student midwife went to fetch a box and some cotton wool to wrap around the baby and protect her from the cold. In spite of the days' heat, nights in the Congo are cold, with treacherous drafts. Another student midwife went to fetch a hot water bottle and stoke up the fire. She returned in distress, for the last hot water bottle had burst as she was filling it. Rubber disintegrates easily in a tropical climate.

They decided to place the baby as close to the fire as they safely could and to have one of the student midwives sleep between the baby and the door to protect her from dangerous drafts.

The following noon as the doctor went to pray with some of the orphanage children, she told them about the baby and also about her little two-year-old sister crying because her mother had died. She explained the difficulties about keeping the little one warm, mentioning the hot water bottle. The baby could so easily die if she got chills. During prayer, one little girl called Ruthie prayed with the blunt conciseness of children: "Dear God, please send us a hot water bottle. It will be no good tomorrow as the baby will be dead, so please send it this afternoon." She added: "And while you are about it, would you please send a little dolly for the baby's sister, so that she will know that you really love her."

The doctor gasped inwardly at the audacity of the prayer, for she knew that the only way it could be answered would be if she received a parcel from her homeland. She had been in Africa for almost four years and never had received a parcel from home. The possibility, further, of someone sending a hot water bottle for use near the equator was remote.

Half way through the afternoon, while teaching in the nurses' training school, she received a message that there was a car at her front door. When she got home, the car had left, but a large twenty-two-pound parcel was sitting on her front porch. She was moved to tears and called for the orphan children to help her open it. There were brightly colored knitted jerseys that she handed out to the excited children. There were knitted bandages for the leprosy patients. There were baking goods — raisins, sultanas. Then, when she put her hand into the parcel again she felt — could it be? She grasped it and pulled it out, a brand new rubber hot water bottle! She cried, for she had not believed that it could possibly happen. Ruthie in the front row rushed forward. "If God sent the hot water bottle, God will also have sent the dolly." She rummaged through the box, and there in the bottom of the box she found it, a beautifully dressed little dolly. "Can I go with you?" she asked, "to give it to the little girl so she'll know that God really loves her?"

The parcel had been on the way for five months, packed up by the doctor's former Sunday school class whose leader was prompted to send a hot water bottle even to the equator. One little girl had given a dolly for an African child five months before the prayer request to bring it that afternoon.[6]

Considerations

Both stories are of interest to us here because our linear understanding of time and space cannot account for what happened. To help the Columbine teenagers in their moment of death two weeks prior to their dying and from hundreds of miles away defies our sequential sense of time as well as our understanding of space. To have one's prayers answered five months before they were spoken, or even before the need for them arose, forces us to contemplate the power of "praying backwards" — an absurdity for linear thinking.

We have in the past tried to explain experiences such as my Benedictine friend's dream by calling them clairvoyant, and we can attribute what happened in the Congo to a meaningful coincidence or to the action of an all-knowing God. Both interpretations are, of course, fine. They teach us little, however, except perhaps to recognize that some people are fortunate, and others have special gifts. But...

- What if time and space are nothing more than simple categories of *our* particular form of consciousness which needs these categories for everyday navigation on the "frequency" where we operate and find meaning?

- What if reality could be understood as so much more, as wider, in fact, and deeper than our ordinary space and time categories can permit?[7]

- What if, as the mystics discovered through direct experience, there is really only the *here* and only *now* —

the divine "presence" and "present" in which the cre-
ative/contemplative mind can in fact participate?[8]

• What if there is nothing that separates us from each
  other and, in fact, from anything?

• What if there is only one whole?

• What if, because all of reality once was one, every particle in the universe now resonates with every other
  particle?

• What if we are all interconnected — with each other, and
  with everything there is — at all times?

• What if some people experience this interconnectedness
  in various ways because of an expansion of consciousness to which all of us may eventually evolve?

• What if thought — and, therefore, prayer and even
  dream time — is energy and can transform reality?

• What if everything that affects me, affects you also and
  does so instantly?

In chapter 4 (see pages 92–94 and endnote 15 on page
189), we reflected on the interconnectedness of the universe — its holographic and organic dimensions — and
how these can affect our sense of God's presence in
our lives.

• What if we were to bring a new sense of divine energy,
  then, into our religious imagination?

• What if we could *see* the cosmic power of creation
  (focused, as Christians believe, through the fullness of
  divine presence in Jesus of Nazareth, a human being "in"

time and space as we are) now also flowing through each one of us who are *non-locally* and *non-temporally* connected to him and to each other?

A mystical perspective, no doubt, filled with extraordinary power and responsibility, and so Danah Zohar (physicist, philosopher, and psychologist) sees it. Speaking of "non-locality" and "non-temporality," she explains: "Things and events once conceived of as separate, parted in both space and time, are seen by the quantum theorist as so integrally linked that their bond mocks the reality of both space and time. They behave, instead, as multiple aspects of some larger whole," from which they receive their energy and meaning.[9] Translating quantum theory into what she calls "quantum psychology," Zohar expands the vision and sees unity and interconnectedness embracing all of us. Whatever each of us does affects all of us directly and instantly, transcending time and space. As each part of our body belongs to one undivided whole, so we belong to each other, but also to our ancestors, and to our progeny, and they to us. "If I injure my hand, my whole body hurts. If I injure my consciousness — fill it with malicious or selfish or evil thoughts — I injure the whole nonlocally connected 'field' of consciousness,"[10] the whole human race, and all of creation.

The responsibility that this view exposes for us calls us to a serious rethinking of the individualism by which, in the past, we so easily could escape the demands of love. Love, however is our essence. "I am responsible for the world," says Zohar, "because, in the words of the late Krishnamurti, 'I am the world.'"[11]

It seems to me that the above "what ifs" greatly expand our perspective on the stories under consideration. If my Benedictine friend experienced depth reality in her dream, we might say that her not being in Littleton at the time of the shooting and the death of the children (given the principle of "action at a distance" or what we have so far identified as "non-locality") would not matter. Nor is time sequence in the second story important. Since all things and all moments touch each other at every point, linear time becomes irrelevant. That my friend did what she did in her dream two weeks earlier does not mean that it could not affect the children at the moment of their deaths. That Ruthie prayed five months later does not mean her prayers did not influence the Sunday school class that sent the parcel. The vision of reality we are reflecting on transcends space and time. There is only *now*, and the past as well as the future — as we experience them in ordinary perception — implode here. In the words of Einstein: "The distinction between past, present, and future is only an illusion."[12] Each of us contains the universe and is connected to every aspect of it at every moment. What quantum calculations reveal is a fundamental reality, a field, of vibrating interconnectedness that is instantaneous. "We and our universe live and breathe in what amounts to a sea of motion — a quantum sea of light."[13] We live in it and belong to it, are part of it and sustained by it.

When referring to human consciousness within the context of quantum physics, Zohar insists:

It becomes impossible to imagine a single aspect of
our lives that is not drawn into one coherent whole.
... The quantum world view transcends the dichot-
omy between mind and matter, or between inner and
outer, by showing us that the basic building blocks
of mind and matter arise out of a common substrate
and are engaged in a mutually creative dialogue whose
roots can be traced back to the very heart of reality
creation.[14]

The source of this vibrating interconnectivity, the "coherent whole" Zohar is referring to, is what physicists refer
to as the "Zero Point Field" — a vast underlying sea of
energy whose existence implies "that all matter in the universe [is] interconnected by waves, which are spread out
through time and space and can carry on to infinity, tying
one part of the universe to every other part."[15]

For many of us these concepts are difficult to grasp, and
perhaps it is best to let them wash over us and allow our
imagination and intuition room to "play" with them. If
we do, they quite often can bring with them unexpected
rewards. For the Christian or Jewish seeker the vision provided here might offer a possible depth explanation for the
"light" which God "spoke" and from which matter was created. The Chinese belief in *qi* and the Indian *prana* may
find support here as well. Brian Swimme offers other terms
for our imagination and reflection — "space-time foam,"
"fecund emptiness," "quantum vacuum" — and a beautiful
reflection on the "all-nourishing-abyss," as a metaphor to
help us approach this "mystery at the base of being"[16]

Animal and Plant World

Perhaps it is good to emphasize, at this point, what we, out of biased human-centeredness, sometimes have a tendency not to notice: Plants and animals also experience reality the way we have attempted to envision it above. They, together with the rest of creation, are interlaced with us and with each other across time and space. Scientific experiments testing animal and plant ESP, for example, show clearly that they experience non-locality. There seems to be a type of "primary perception" here that transcends all recognized boundaries.

III

Cleve Backster, director of the Backster School of Lie Detection, used his highly perfected devices to test conscious reactions of underwater plants. He found that plants not only have a form of consciousness but exhibit empathy as well. They were deeply "stressed," for example, when baby shrimp were killed in the surrounding area. Nothing could stop their reaction, according to Backster, not even lead shields hiding, and distancing them from, the killing.

Backster became interested in this research when he "accidentally discovered that laboratory plants reacted to the cracking of eggs. He then began investigating the sensitivity of eggs themselves, and to his astonishment found that they also showed evidence of primary perception." He carried his research all the way to cell cultures, amoebas, mold cultures, and blood samples. His experiments led him to conclude "that total memory may go down to a single-cell level, at least."[17]

Considerations

Even the line between organic and inorganic matter has become blurred. Language is inadequate to describe the dynamics of life. As Nobel-laureate physicist Max Born said, "We distinguish between living and dead matter: between moving bodies and bodies at rest. This is a *primitive point of view.* What seems dead, a stone or the proverbial doornail, say, is actually forever in motion. We have merely become accustomed to judge by outward appearances; by the deceptive impressions we get through our senses. We shall have to learn to describe things in new and better ways."[18]

By way of an aside, and to connect us once again to the theme of this chapter, it may be good to point out here that our senses give to us exactly what we are *trained* to expect. Children, in other words, are "educated" to *see* the world as they do and to *"learn* to ignore certain aspects of their reality that are considered hallucinatory by the adults around them."[19] As Jean Piaget has aptly demonstrated: the ability to perceive is innate; *what* we perceive is learned.[20] This explains why, even with all the research and discoveries asking for it, a changing world perspective is so difficult to achieve. It threatens us, and we can easily perceive those who present it to us as dangerous and, when it pertains to religious interpretations, even as evil.

What if reality could be understood as so much more, as wider, in fact, and deeper than our ordinary space and time categories can permit?

Primary Perception

IV

"Primary perception" between animals, especially in the manifestation of empathy, can be profoundly moving. A mother rabbit and her litter were tested years ago in the Soviet Union. Her babies were taken from her, placed into a deeply submerged submarine, and killed at specific times. The mother, kept under surveillance in a laboratory on land and miles away, reacted each time one of the babies was killed, although she had no contact and no possible way of knowing.[21]

V

Amazing stories have surfaced lately about animal communication with humans, and vice versa. Among these, the stories of elephants are numerous. The help afforded humans by elephants during the 2004 tsunami disaster, for example, is truly extraordinary.

Reporting on John Green, a forty-three-year-old Canadian hazardous materials specialist helping out in Indonesia, the *Ottawa Sun* (February 7, 2005) gave his account of the use of elephants in locating bodies in the wreckage and devastation left behind by the tsunami: "When an elephant came across a body buried under piles of debris, it placed its trunk on the ground and swayed gently back and forth. 'What is unbelievable, is that you could see tears welling up in the elephant's eyes,' said Green. 'And every time they would find a body.'"

VI

In her book *The Healing Light*, Agnes Sanford tells the
following story:

> A certain engineer was once surveying in a field when
> a bull charged his party with lowered head and thun-
> dering hoofs. There was no tree to climb. There was
> no fence to jump. So the engineer stood his ground,
> filled his mind with the love of God and projected it
> to the bull.
>
> "I am God's man and you are God's bull," he
> thought in silence. "God made both of us, and in
> the name of Jesus Christ I say that there is nothing
> but loving kindness between us."
>
> The bull stopped abruptly. For a moment he looked
> about uncertainly, as if confused. Then he wandered
> off and lay down peacefully under a bush. And
> all that day as the men prospected in the field he
> grazed quietly behind them, as if he enjoyed their
> presence.
>
> "Will you tell me what you did to that bull?" asked
> a farm boy who was holding the rod for the surveyor.
> "That was a mad bull if I ever saw one. *Will you tell
> me what you did to him?*" ("I can believe every story in
> that book except the one about the bull," a lady once
> said to me. But the engineer was my brother, and the
> story is true.)[22]

Thought Is Energy

I suggested earlier that thought is energy and can transform reality, as in fact it transformed the behavior of the bull in the story above. Much experimentation has been done in the field of medicine to test the results of prayer in this regard, and I have written on this topic in my book *Prayer and the Quest for Healing: On Personal Transformation and Cosmic Responsibility.* But, as Danah Zohar observes, ordinary day-to-day thinking as well — human consciousness generally — can be transformative even as it can be destructive. We need to take responsibility for our thoughts.

The writings of Christiane Northrup, M.D., are perhaps some of the most remarkable testaments to this at the present time. In a letter she wrote to her friends[23] shortly before the second Gulf War, she is very specific:

> The fear and anxiety caused by war are the biggest health challenges we face right now. As a physician, I know full well that emotions such as fear and anger impede the healing process and, if held long enough, actually lock us into a vicious cycle that produces more pain, more fear, and more anxiety. This can wreak havoc in our minds, bodies, and spirits. But this does not have to be the case.

Northrup identifies a number of ways we can help ourselves, the most important of which is probably the suggestion that we become aware of the power of thought.

Because of the law of attraction, negative thoughts — discouragement, anger, condemnation, or what she calls an "embattled mentality" — only serve to build up the power of the agents of war and to give increase to the circumstances that gave rise to the negativity to begin with. We simply empower the very people whose actions we find harmful and offensive in the first place.

To create peace and kindness, we need to be peaceful and kind. Northrup actually suggests that we intentionally spend some time several times a day envisioning our circumstances, or even the world as a whole, as peaceful, free, happy, and "life-centered." We use our imagination, in other words, to create (virtually) the reality we long for.

I would encourage us to add an act of thanksgiving at the end of this time of visioning, with trust-filled confidence that good will ultimately prevail. Sending light to the person or group of persons who cause the pain and disharmony, the war and oppression, surrounding them with God's peace and with the wish that they achieve the highest potential of their humanity actually helps transform them. Surrounding ourselves with light and filling our own minds with positive thoughts also lightens our own energy field and changes our vibrations. In other words, we become the light we are sending out.

VII

One can easily regard suggestions such as these as wishful thinking or, at best, prayerful hope. Numerous studies, however, conducted not primarily by religious leaders but by the scientific and medical community, attest to their efficacy. Lynne McTaggart in her book *The Field: The Quest for the Secret Force of the Universe* (chapter 10, "The Healing Field"), recounts a number of them, most notably perhaps the study of the long-distance healing of severely sick AIDS patients, conducted by Elisabeth Targ (psychiatrist) and Fred Sicher (research psychologist) under the strictest protocol.

The selected long-distance healers were for the most part of widely diverse religious backgrounds. Some had been trained in what McTaggart identified as "non-religious healing schools." During the six-month period allowed for the experiment 40 percent of the control population died, but at the end of the study all in the healing group "were not only still alive but had become healthier, on the basis of their own reports and medical evaluations."[24]

VIII

An extraordinary story of a child's "primary perception" that invites us to broaden our view of human ways of knowing beyond the cognitive abilities of the brain is recounted by Paul Pearsall in his book *The Heart's Code: Tapping the Wisdom and Power of Our Heart Energy.* He tells of an eight-year-old recipient of a heart transplant from a ten-year-old murder victim. The recipient began to have nightmares recalling the murder of her donor, was eventually able to lead the police to the murderer, and, due to the exact information regarding time, weapon, place, and clothes worn by the murderer, helped secure his conviction.[25]

The existence of cellular consciousness and memory are exciting and relatively recent scientific discoveries, phrased perhaps most radically in what until recently was considered "heretical" speculation: "Consciousness [is] a global phenomenon that [occurs] everywhere in the body and not simply in our brains."[26] Or in the words of Deepak Chopra, M.D., "Every cell is a little sentient being. Sitting in the liver or heart or kidney, it 'knows' everything you do, but in its own fashion."[27]

Consciousness and Light

Equally exciting is the realization that what consciousness is, light is also: "Consciousness has no place and no shape. It is invisible yet illuminates everything. It is unimpeded by time and space."[28] So is light. Light is virtually omnipresent but invisible. Although we think we perceive it, we actually only see its reflection on objects. Outer space is filled with light, yet to the human eye there is only a deep, deep darkness.[29] Light is there when all possible other "objects" even the smallest subatomic particles are removed, and the scientist is convinced that she or he has achieved a perfect vacuum.[30]

What is of significance to us regarding these findings is the possible link between consciousness and light. Actually the notion should not really be surprising at all, since, in common parlance, we almost seem to take this link for granted. A person of high intelligence is referred to as "bright" or even "brilliant." When we do not understand something, we ask to be "enlightened," or "illuminated," or to have someone "shed some light" on the matter we are struggling with. We identify someone who lacks an inquisitive mind as "dull." When we are not informed we complain of "being kept in the dark."

Over the years, the verification of Fritz Albert Popp's original research has shown that cells emit light and that "consciousness, at its most basic, [is] coherent light."[31] Christian Wertenbaker speculates meaningfully in this regard:

> While the physiological basis of consciousness is not yet understood, recent evidence indicates that it may depend on *electromagnetic vibrations — light,* though not in the visible range — involving significant portions of the nervous system. The degree of vibratory correlation between different portions of the nervous system *may correspond to levels of consciousness:* in a relatively automatic mode of functioning, smaller portions of the brain may share electromagnetic vibrations [light] sufficiently to process information needed for routine thinking and moving, *while in a state of greater awareness there may be a more generalized harmony of vibrations [light] in the brain or even the whole body.*[32]

Putting the above discussion into a simple context, we may want to ponder whether the haloes that religious artists have painted, for centuries now, around the heads of saints (most prominently around the head of Jesus), and the light surrounding portrayals of important figures in Eastern religions as well, are not, in fact, more than merely artistic ways of indicating their holiness and "enlightenment." In my book *In the Stillness You Will Know*, reflecting on my friend Clare's dying, I suggested that perhaps:

> our bodies are simply light's radiation locus throughout the years of our life and that, because of that, we truly are "children of Light." Do we move beyond or out of ourselves when we die, staying, nevertheless, connected to everything? . . . Are the "inner light of the spirit" and the "outer light" that radiates through the stars one and the same, then? Is consciousness the "light" gift that we bring to our sojourn here on earth: "to know like a lover, so that one becomes one with the cosmos reflecting it . . . back to itself."[33]

Our considerations here might lead us to say yes to much of this. The wonder and amazing paradox of it all seems to be that matter as a whole is, at its simplest — "viewed from the microscopic level . . . *frozen light*,"[34] which, as "photon," however, has no mass, extension, or solidity, that is, none of the normal, unambiguous, and irreducible attributes of matter.[35]

On Being Channels of Light

IX

In his autobiography, Jacques Lusseyran, blind hero of the French Resistance during World War II, tells of his amazing encounter with a *deep inner light* that came to him at the age of eight, shortly after he had been permanently blinded in an accident.

He had very sensitive parents who encouraged him, immediately after his accident, to move back into the world and try to encounter it anew. He remembers feeling enormous frustration, since his usual methods of encounter no longer worked for him. Space no longer felt or responded to him in the way he remembered. Nothing seemed familiar, and he felt totally helpless.

Then, he says, something made him change his way of *seeing*. Instead of turning his sight toward the world outside, he began to look more closely at a world within — "from an inner place to one further within." And he became aware of "a radiance emanating from a place [he] knew nothing about, a place which might as well have been outside [him] as within."[36] He felt indescribable relief, for the reality of the experience took hold of him and joy came back into his life:

> The amazing thing was that this was not magic for me at all, but reality. I could no more have denied it than people with eyes can deny that they see.... I bathed in [the light].... I could feel light rising, spreading, resting on objects, giving them form, then leaving them.
>
> Withdrawing or diminishing is what I mean, for the opposite of light was never present.... At every waking hour and even in my dreams I lived in a stream of light.[37]

The experience was so far beyond his comprehension that on occasion, in an attempt to test it, he would try to deny it and make an effort not to see the light. At night he would lower his eyelids and tell himself that there was no light. But with serenity and calm — like a lake in the evening when all is still — the light was there. When he gathered all his will power to try to stop the flow, all he would experience is a small disturbance for a brief moment — something like a whirlpool, but even that was flooded with light. He remembers feeling anguish doing this. It seemed to him that he needed light to live as much as he needed air.

The light did dim, however, on occasion — sometimes almost to the point of vanishing. It happened whenever he allowed fear to take over his trust and confidence, when he doubted his capacity to walk freely in his surroundings and encounter his world with equanimity. His surroundings then became as hostile as he had feared, and he would invariably hurt himself. He was, in the true sense of the word, "blinded by fear." Anger and impatience had the same result, as did ambition — wanting to be first at all costs — jealousy, and unfriendliness. When he allowed these feelings to take over, it seemed to him as if "a bandage came down over [his] eyes and [he] was bound hand and foot and cast aside. All of a sudden a black hole opened, and [he] was helplessly inside."[38] When he was serene, however, and trusting, with open confidence toward the world, he as well as his whole world were bathed in light, as if "existing through it and because of it."[39]

Lusseyran continues his discussion with a fascinating reflection on sounds. He experienced them like he experienced light: as neither inside nor outside — as, in fact, "a real presence" passing through him. "There was the sound, its echo, and another sound into which the first sound melted and to which it had given birth. . . . With sound I never came to an end, for this was another kind of infinite."[40]

Objects too seemed alive to Lusseyran. They vibrated and called for a response, for connection, for relationship. He could identify where the trees were along the road he was walking. By holding himself in a kind of reposed attentiveness, he could feel their vibrations. In that way reality came toward him and left its impression on him. He became, as it were, part of the things he encountered, and they of him:

> Touching the tomatoes in the garden, and really touching them, touching the walls of the house, the materials of the curtains or a clod of earth is surely seeing them as fully as eyes can see. But it is more than seeing them, it is turning in on them and allowing the current they hold to connect with one's own, like electricity. To put it differently, this means an end of living in front of things and a beginning of living with them. Never mind if the word sounds shocking, for this is love.[41]

There is here an exchange of energy, an at-oneness, that is close to the mystical. Inside of him, Lusseyran says, "every sound, every scent, and every shape was forever changing into light, and light itself changing into color."[42]

The condition for this experience, quite simply, was one of humility and attentive receptivity; a condition of "releasement," of letting go of ego and surrendering, as well as empowering; an acceptance of what is *as* it is, without any attempt to control and dominate. This disposition helped Lusseyran throughout his life and especially allowed him to survive the Nazi concentration camp at Buchenwald, where he was imprisoned during the Second World War for his Resistance activities. No trickery or ruse can save one in such horror, only a deep inner centeredness — a faith, says Lusseyran, "that has its roots in our very being, that in time has become our very self."[43] He was one of two thousand French prisoners there, of whom only thirty survived:

> All of us, whether we are blind or not, are terribly greedy. We want things only for ourselves. Even without realizing it, we want the universe to be like us and give us all the room in it. But a blind child learns very quickly that this cannot be. He has to learn it, for every time he forgets that he is not alone in the world he strikes against an object, hurts himself and is called to order. But each time he remembers he is rewarded, for everything comes his way.[44]

Considerations

This lengthy story opens up, it seems to me, an experiential reality of light and consciousness that is beyond mathematics and the laboratory as such. One senses benevolence here and a being drawn to authenticity. We get, as it were, a sense of something larger, something beyond us that is nevertheless intimately one with us. The scientists on whose findings and theories we have been reflecting would call it a type of "organized energy field" in which the light originates. It is, they claim, holographic in nature and, therefore, is contained in, and informs, every part of us even as it also surrounds us and holds us.

One of the first to study this phenomenon was Harold S. Burr at Yale University. His research into the electrical fields (the auras or organized energy fields) around numerous organisms (in this case tiny seedlings) led him to discover that the field around each seedling did not, in fact, take the shape of the tiny sprout but, surprisingly, resembled instead the adult form of the plant. Burr's data led him to postulate that any developing organism seems "destined to follow a prescribed growth template." It has, in other words, a *destiny* which is already present in and to the organism, appears around it in the form of light, and is drawing it toward its own perfection. Burr concluded that this growth template originates from the individual "electromagnetic field" — "bioenergetic growth field," "bioenergy field" — of the organism.[45]

What is fascinating here is that the field Burr discovered identified the "future" of the seedling in the present. It surrounded the sprout as its aura, its "field of light," and (because of its holographic nature) was contained in each tiny cell as well, "calling" it to *become what it already was*.[46]

The field, then, is larger and beyond the tiny plant and, at the same time, within every part of it.

One can extrapolate from this and suggest that what Burr discovered is true of all living organisms. We can suggest further, perhaps, that Lusseyran had the extraordinary visual, moral, and affective "experience" of this field in the form of light, that he was given *recognition* of it as it pertains to humans and was enabled to interpret it for us.

Passing into the Light

X

The universe is an amazing event of light, and in us this light has come to consciousness. Though, to this date, none of the scientific questing has plumbed the depth of light's mystery, it graces us with its presence, nevertheless, and lures us on into deeper reflection.

In the mid-1980s, while researching the vow of poverty and its invitation to "let go," to empty oneself of all ego concerns and become open and vulnerable, I came upon a story in Donald Nichol's book *Holiness* that touched me deeply. Nichol had discovered the story in Chogyam Trungpa's book *Born in Tibet*. It tells of a saintly old man in northeastern Tibet, known particularly for his extraordinary compassion. When the man came close to death, he asked as his last and only request that his body not be buried for eight days. He had been a tall man, but to those who carried his body to a back room to remain there for a week after he had died, the body already appeared to be shrinking. This seemed to continue and puzzled his family when they came to look at his body during the week. On the eighth day, to their astonishment, his body had vanished. The family went for advice to a learned local lama, who told them that, in fact, similar happenings had been reported a number of times in the past. "The body of the saintly man had been absorbed into the Light."[47]

Nichol told this story, paralleling it with an account of the cosmic event of "black holes." In both instances, he suggested, there is total absorption. According to modern astronomy, a star or even a whole universe can suddenly contract, becoming increasingly dense and, in turn, accelerating the contraction. "Eventually this increasing density produces such a curvature of matter that the universe passes beyond perception, leaving a black hole."[48] Certain theories suggest that the universe will eventually reappear elsewhere in the cosmos, possibly in the form of quasars emitting immense quantities of light.[49] Nichol stresses the similarity "between the course of events in the visible cosmos and the course of events in a [person's] spiritual life. That course is the way of contraction, of concentration to the point at which one vanishes."[50] I want to add: One vanishes — only to be turned into light — to be absorbed into Light.

I found Nichol's story fascinating when I first read it, and over the years I have used it in numerous lectures as an analogy for the call to "evangelical poverty." Recently, however, the story reappeared in my life in a much more real and contemporary way and left me to question my analogical use of it. In a 2002 publication of the

Institute of Noetic Sciences (IONS), Gail Bernice Holland writes about Benedictine brother David Steindl-Rast, who had approached IONS to propose an investigation into a "phenomenon in which the corpses of highly developed spiritual individuals reputedly vanish within days of death."[51] Steindl-Rast was referring here to Tibetan masters known particularly for their compassion. Sometimes it is reported that after their death and their vanishing they appear again to trusted friends and relatives. Often light, in the colors of the rainbow,[52] appears in the sky and over their dwellings during the dying process and especially after their death.

Steindl-Rast's interest in these reports was aroused because he felt that the stories touched the roots of his faith in the resurrection of Jesus, who also was a man of deep compassion and whose body, too, was said to have vanished shortly after his entombment. He also is believed to have appeared to his followers after his "disappearance":

> In today's world, Steindl-Rast points out, the resurrection of Jesus Christ is interpreted differently, depending upon one's spiritual leanings. For fundamentalists, the resurrection — the act of rising from the dead — happened only to Jesus, and couldn't happen to any other human. The minimalists, on the other hand, ... focus on Jesus' spirit living on, and believe that the resurrection had nothing to do with his body.
>
> Yet a large number of people (including myself) are open to the concept that the body, too, is significant in

the spiritual realm, *and that certain spiritual experiences are universal.*[53]

Steindl-Rast enlisted the help of Father Francis Tiso — a Roman Catholic priest familiar with Tibetan culture and language.[54] As it happened, Tiso was on his way to Tibet and, once there, explored the rainbow body phenomenon through extensive interviews with eyewitnesses and other Tibetan masters (among others: Lama Sonam Gyamtso, Lama A-chos, and Lama Norta). As it turned out, they had recently experienced the rainbow body phenomenon in one of their lamas, and their memories were alive and fresh.

In 1998 Khenpo A-chos, a Gelugpa monk of Khams, Tibet, known for his faithfulness and integrity, purity of life, extraordinary compassion, and transformative effect on others had died:

A few days before Khenpo A-chos died, a rainbow appeared directly above his hut. After he died, there were dozens of rainbows in the sky.... According to eyewitnesses, after his breath stopped his flesh became kind of pinkish.... All said it began to shine.

Lama A-chos suggested wrapping his friend's body in a yellow robe, the type all Gelug monks wear. As the days passed, they maintained they could see, through the robe, that his bones and his body were shrinking....

After seven days, they removed the yellow cloth, and no body remained. Lama Norta and a few other individuals claimed that after his death Khenpo A-chos appeared to them in visions and dreams.[55]

Considerations

It is important to note that the event cited here, as strange
as it may appear to us, is (even if rare) really not unique to
Khenpo A-chos. Tiso's research shows, in fact, that documentation of bodies shrinking or disappearing shortly
after death existed centuries ago.[56] The importance of these
occurrences for Tiso, as well as Steindl-Rast, lies not in
their extraordinariness, especially to the Western mind, but
primarily in what they reveal about spiritual practices (in
particular, the embodiment of compassion and love), and
what light they might shed on human nature itself — "the
expansion of human consciousness and our potential as
human beings."[57]

Both men realize, of course, that their research is controversial both in the world of religion as well as that of
science, where much more documentation and verification
will be required. Aside from such matters as the existence
of life after death, immortality, and reincarnation that this
research raises, certainly the most important for Christian
interests is in what insights it might give us into the resurrection of Jesus, his ascension, and the assumption of his
mother. It is clear, as Gail Bernice Holland from IONS observes, that "the rainbow body is a complex phenomenon
that will take years of study," but, as Steindl-Rast suggests,
"If we can establish as an anthropological fact, . . . that what
is described in the resurrection of Jesus has not only happened to others, but is happening today, it would put our
view of human potential in a completely different light."[58]
In "A Lecture on the Resurrection in Reference to the

Rainbow Body Phenomenon," given at the Presidio Chapel in San Francisco, on December 12, 2001, Tiso states the religious interest well: "So our claims about the reality of the resurrection and of the post-mortem disappearance of bodies of yogins with various displays of spiritual attainment seem to be telling us something both old and new, of our past and, most importantly, of our barely imagined future."[59]

In the same lecture he relates his amazement that speaking candidly of this phenomenon and its implications with both friends and parishioners has proved most rewarding — confirming their faith rather than threatening it. After one of his lectures in a New York parish a man came up to him full of enthusiasm: "The rainbow body," he insisted, "the body of light, and the resurrection are all interrelated and perhaps the same thing, based on the same teachings and practices, and they are of immediate importance to every human being who is spiritually committed and aware of the fact of death."[60]

There is no doubt, nevertheless, that some will be threatened by this discussion, especially if their belief structure demands exclusiveness and, by that fact, a need to be unique and even superior to other religions. To hear that what happened to Jesus can happen to others somehow threatens the uniqueness of Jesus for them and questions his divinity. None of this, however, needs to happen.

I stressed in chapter 4 that all of us belong to a cosmic family whose interconnectedness is Love. I suggested that this Love empowers the perpetual transformation of all things. In this chapter I mentioned that light seems to be the basic, primordial reality of the universe, and that matter (frozen light) and energy (light) are interchangeable; that our bodies are simply light's radiation locus while we are here on earth (I prefer to say on this frequency[61]). The notion, therefore, of holy ones turning back into light after their death — possibly being absorbed into their auric field (radiating it in the form of rainbow colors), and thence moving ever further into the sacred Light/Love that pulsates and radiates throughout the cosmos — should not be so difficult to accept. Having fulfilled their destiny, they return whence they came. Tiso, explaining Eastern teaching, puts it simply: "Full realization is when all phenomena *return to their source*."[62]

From a Christian-mystical point of view, could we perhaps see this as (their body, that is, "matter") being absorbed into Spirit? As Teilhard de Chardin would say to help us along with this understanding: "Concretely speaking, there is no matter and spirit; rather there exists only *matter that is becoming spirit* [Light]. The stuff of the universe is spirit-matter."[63] And the rainbow body exemplifies this becoming, this transformation for us. Might we perhaps add: as did the resurrection-ascension of Jesus, the assumption of Mary, and, in the scriptures, the passage of Elijah (2 Kings 2:11) and Enoch (Heb. 11:5)?

These are profound questions that remain largely unaddressed as yet, in part because they seem to threaten how we for centuries have interpreted the experience of Jesus' followers after his death. These interpretations originated in the context of the time in which they were written, with the only view of the world the interpreters could have had and could have used for their understanding and faith-articulation. It is a view that has been operative in our tradition ever since Christianity was formulated. Even though, through the years, there have been internal, but not essential, changes to what has come to be called "dualism," the essentially dualistic formulation of Christian beliefs has never had to encounter a radically other perspective until now.

Today, as I have mentioned, this view is imploding in the light of scientific discoveries. This chapter was an attempt to offer a simple perspective on some of these discoveries in the hope of providing the possibility for re-visioning some of our interpretations of the Christ event, and of thus enhancing its meaningfulness and its relevance for today.

Steindl-Rast and Tiso are clearly Christian men of faith who, nevertheless, do not shy away from what "offers itself" in our day for our reflection. They do this, I believe, out of respect and love, and within the context of the freedom that comes with knowing that the Mystery is never exhausted and ever draws us into its tender and yet awe-full embrace. We can do no less.

Conclusion

I frequently bring a large photograph of an iceberg to my lectures these days. It beautifully depicts the large white mass of ice against the blue of sky and sea, but it also (by some photographic maneuvering) allows us to see the enormous and much, much larger mass of ice that lies hidden below the surface of the ocean. The picture symbolizes our perpetual struggle with what we see, as well as with an awareness of the much more significant mystery that seems ever to remain hidden from our view.

It is so easy to remain with the first, to understand reality that way, and to absolutize it for ourselves. But as seekers we do so only at the risk of self-betrayal and ultimate boredom and despair. Many of us do have a choice still, but the mystics among us do not. They are, if you will, compelled to stand in the tension of the two options, for they *have glimpsed into the mystery* and can no longer resist the vision:

All at once, without warning of any kind, I found myself wrapped in a flame-colored cloud. For an instant I thought of fire, an immense conflagration somewhere . . . the next, I knew that the fire was within myself. Directly afterward there came upon me a sense of exultation, of immense joyousness accompanied or immediately followed by an intellectual illumination impossible to describe. Among other things, I did not merely come to believe, but I *saw* that the universe is not composed of dead matter, but is, on the contrary, a *living Presence;* I became conscious in myself of eternal life. It was not a conviction that I would have eternal life, but a consciousness that I possessed eternal life then; I *saw* that all [human beings] are immortal; that the cosmic order is such that without any peradventure all things work together for the good of each and all; that the foundation principle of the world, of all the worlds, is what we call *love,* and that the happiness of each and all is in the long run absolutely certain. . . . I *knew* that what this vision showed was true. I had attained to a point of view from which I *saw* that it must be true. That view, that conviction, I may say that *consciousness,* has never, even during periods of deepest depression, been lost.[64]

Thoughts and Questions for Meditation

What are your thoughts concerning the following selections from chapter 5?

1. We are today being invited, according to Zajonc, into a transformation that requires of us a new set of inner and outer eyes as well. We need these to help us transcend what he calls "cultural determinants which bias us toward seeing the world in certain ways." We are being called to *see* new things.

2. Clearly there are a number of ways to help prepare us for necessary re-visioning; for movement toward reappropriating the charter events of our religion and regaining a sense of wonder and of depth faith so easily lost through "factualism" and the excessive logic and intellectualism of the past. My hope in this chapter is to do so by means of reflecting on stories — true events that have occurred during the last several years. They have led me to take seriously the convergence of disciplines that invites a change in perspective. They also have helped me not to be afraid of paradox in

my life, but to come to expect it and to accept it as a given in the world of reality. They have encouraged me, therefore, to accept what is often referred to as the "paranormal" and to begin to see it as perhaps normal instead — as a way of stretching us beyond the narrow confines of our here and now, a way of giving us a deeper realization of the still dormant powers within many of us.

3. What was your reaction to stories 1 and 2? And to the "what if" questions following the stories (pages 111–113) and offered for your consideration?

4. Whatever each of us does affects all of us directly and instantly, transcending time and space. As each part of our body belongs to one undivided whole, so we belong to each other, but also to our ancestors, and to our progeny, and they to us. "If I injure my hand, my whole body hurts. If I injure my consciousness — fill it with malicious or selfish or evil thoughts — I injure the whole nonlocally connected 'field' of consciousness," the whole human race, and all of creation.

5. The source of this vibrating interconnectivity, the "coherent whole," is what physicists refer to as the "Zero Point Field" — a vast underlying sea of energy whose existence implies "that all matter in the universe is interconnected by waves, which are spread out through time and space and can carry on to infinity, tying one part of the universe to every other part." For many of us these concepts are difficult to grasp, and perhaps it is best to let them wash over us and allow our

imagination and intuition room to "play" with them. If we do, they quite often can bring with them unexpected rewards. For the Christian or Jewish seeker the vision provided here might offer a possible depth explanation for the "light" which God "spoke" and from which matter was created. The Chinese belief in *qi* and the Indian *prana* may find support here as well. Brian Swimme offers other terms for our imagination and reflection — "space-time foam," "fecund emptiness," "quantum vacuum" — and a beautiful reflection on the "all-nourishing-abyss," as a metaphor to help us approach this "mystery at the base of being"

6. Plants and animals also experience reality the way we have attempted to envision it above. They, together with the rest of creation, are interlaced with us and with each other across time and space. Scientific experiments testing animal and plant ESP, for example, show clearly that they experience non-locality. There seems to be a type of "primary perception" here that transcends all recognized boundaries.

7. From Marilyn Ferguson: Even the line between organic and inorganic matter has become blurred. Language is inadequate to describe the dynamics of life. As Nobel-laureate physicist Max Born said, "We distinguish between living and dead matter: between moving bodies and bodies at rest. This is a *primitive point of view.* What seems dead, a stone or the proverbial doornail, say, is actually forever in motion. We have merely

become accustomed to judge by outward appearances; by the deceptive impressions we get through our senses. We shall have to learn to describe things in new and better ways."

8. Thought is energy and can transform reality. Much experimentation has been done in the field of medicine to test the result of prayer in this regard. But, as Danah Zohar observes, ordinary day-to-day thinking as well — human consciousness generally — can be transformative even as it can be destructive. We need to take responsibility for our thoughts.

9. Because of the law of attraction, negative thoughts — discouragement, anger, condemnation, or what Christiane Northrup calls an "embattled mentality" — only serve to build up the power of the agents of war and to give increase to the circumstances that gave rise to the negativity to begin with. We simply empower the very people whose actions we find harmful and offensive in the first place. To create peace and kindness, we need to be peaceful and kind. Northrup actually suggests that we intentionally spend some time several times a day envisioning our circumstances, or even the world as a whole, as peaceful, free, happy, and "life-centered." We use our imagination, in other words, to create (virtually) the reality we long for. I would encourage us to add an act of thanksgiving at the end of this time of visioning, with trust-filled confidence that good will ultimately prevail. Sending light

to the person or group of persons who cause the pain and disharmony, the war and oppression, surrounding them with God's peace and with the wish that they achieve the highest potential of their humanity actually helps transform them.

10. Consider "consciousness as light" (page 124). The entire section invites reflection and a major paradigm shift.

11. What are your thoughts about the Jacques Lusseyran story (page 126–30)? How does it affect your relationship to yourself and your surroundings?

12. The universe is an amazing event of light, and in us this light has come to consciousness. Though, to this date, none of the scientific questing has plumbed the depth of light's mystery, it graces us with its presence, nevertheless, and lures us on into deeper reflection. What is your reaction to the "rainbow body phenomenon"? Does it frighten you or excite you?

13. Respond to the following citations from Tiso and Gerber respectively:

    • "So our claims about the reality of the resurrection and of the post-mortem disappearance of bodies of yogins with various displays of spiritual attainment seem to be telling us something both old and new, of our past and, most importantly, of our barely imagined future."

    • "We are multidimensional beings. We are more than just flesh and bones, cells and proteins. We are beings in dynamic equilibrium with a universe of energy and light of many different frequencies and forms. We are composed of the stuff of the universe which, as we have already discovered, is actually 'frozen light.' Mystics throughout the ages have referred to us as beings of light. It is only now that science has begun to validate the basic premise behind this statement."

14. The notion, therefore, of holy ones turning back into light after their death — possibly being absorbed into their auric field (radiating it in the form of rainbow colors), and thence moving ever further into the sacred Light/Love that pulsates and radiates throughout the cosmos — should not be so difficult to accept. Having fulfilled their destiny, they return whence they came. Tiso, explaining Eastern teaching, puts it simply: "Full realization is when all phenomena return to their source." From the Christian-mystical point of view, could we perhaps see this as (their body, that is, "matter") being absorbed into Spirit? As Teilhard de Chardin would say to help us along with this understanding: "Concretely speaking, there is no matter and spirit; rather there exists only matter that is becoming spirit [Light]. The stuff of the universe is spirit-matter." And the rainbow body exemplifies this becoming, this transformation for us. Might we perhaps add: as did the resurrection-ascension of Jesus, the assumption of Mary, and, in the scriptures, the passage of Elijah (2 Kings 2:11) and Enoch (Heb. 11:5)?

Walking into the Story

Let yourself receive the one
who is opening to you so deeply.
For if we genuinely love Him,
we wake up inside Christ's body . . .

and everything that is hurt, everything
that seemed to us dark, harsh, shameful,
maimed, ugly, irreparably
damaged, is in Him transformed

and recognized as whole, as lovely,
and radiant in His light
we awaken as the Beloved
in every part of our body.

— Simeon, the New Theologian,
949–1022 CE

Leading the Way

The story is told of an old monk who one night in a dream was visited by the risen Christ. They went on a walk together in quiet intimacy, enjoying each other's presence. Finally the old man turned to Jesus and asked: "When you walked the hills of Palestine, you mentioned that one day you would come again in all your glory. Lord, it's been so long; when will you return for good?"

After a few moments of silence the resurrected and living One said, "When my presence in nature all around you and my presence beneath the surface of your skin is as real to you as my presence right now, when this awareness becomes second nature to you, *then* will I have returned for good."

The dream was very vivid and carried the monk into the next day when, deep in thought, he walked again, this time by himself — or so he thought. As he stopped and bent over a small pond to wash his face, he gazed "for a brief but eternal moment" at his reflection and at the images of the trees and the sky reflected in the water as well, and there he heard a gentle whisper: "You are my beloved son, in whom I am well pleased."[1]

◆ ◆ ◆

"Walking into the Story" means surrendering to its deepest truth. It means accepting it as our charter, our reality, whose gathering point and healing symbol for all Christians is ever Christ Jesus, "leading us with relentless love into conversion: at-onement with our inmost being and through this, mysteriously, with the universe as well."[2] I wrote these words many years ago for the classes I was teaching at the time. Today they are still true for me, but, oh, they mean so much more!

The reflections and "invitations to wonder" in the preceding chapters have been my way of preparing for the question that demands today, perhaps more so than it has ever done through the ages, a deeply personal, a heart-searing response: *Who do you say I am?* If, indeed, faith is primarily what I have attempted to describe in chapter 2, catechism answers to this question, as clear and comprehensive as they may be, are not enough anymore. At best, they speak to the belief-expressions of the ages, formulated for the ages. We owe them respect. But unless *I* can touch the depth of *my* ache and find a response there that lures me, the desert will ultimately swallow me up and wither not only my bones but my heart and every thought in my head as well.

Courage to Face the Unknown

Who is Jesus Christ for us today, and who is his God? As much as has been written about Jesus, there is precious little we know as historical fact. It is not my intention, nor am I qualified, to take up the highly specialized and complex field of scripture scholarship here and offer my own opinion. Though I find it fascinating to study the writings concerning Christian scriptures (that is, their origin, their diverse and sometimes contradictory renditions, the eventual "canonization" of some and exclusion and even destruction of others, new discoveries of ancient texts and how they reveal a past long considered as closed to us), I have no desire or authority to write on this subject; nor does it relate directly to the intention of this book or this chapter.[3]

Suffice it, then, to say simply, and merely for the purpose of freeing up our reflections on the Story:

- We do not have the "originals" of any of the books that came to be included in the New Testament, or indeed of any Christian book from antiquity.

- "What we have," Bart Ehrman assures us, "are copies of the originals or, to be more accurate, copies made from copies of the copies of the copies of the originals. Most of these surviving copies are hundreds of years removed from the originals,"[4] which themselves were written long after the events themselves.

- Comparative studies today show that, depending on the scribes who worked on them through the centuries, and their communities' particular interpretation of the matters being copied, the writings were often considerably modified.

- The majority of contemporary scholars agree, furthermore, that the Gospels were written not by the historical figures whose name they bear, but "by otherwise unknown but relatively well-educated Greek-speaking (and writing) Christians during the second half of the first century."[5]

- Students of the Christian past are aware also, though it may not be generally known, that early Christianity was anything but unanimous in its beliefs. The divinity of Jesus, his knowledge of his divinity, his death and the reason for it, and the meaning of redemption are only some of numerous topics that were widely debated in antiquity.

Who was and is Jesus of Nazareth? Who is the God he witnessed to and made present to us?

Bart Ehrman cannot be more direct: "During the first three Christian centuries, the practices and beliefs found among people who called themselves Christians were so varied that the differences between Roman Catholics, Primitive Baptists, and Seventh-Day Adventists pale by comparison."[6]

As I mentioned in chapter 3 ("The Burden of the Past") much of the disagreement came to an end, around the first decades of the fourth century with the ascendancy of orthodox Christianity and the formation of organized religion under hierarchical rule and imperial protection. What became the "body of faith" after that was quickly and firmly proclaimed throughout the empire and was soon understood as "original" to the vision and words of Jesus. In the absence of historical records and the non-existence of our modern penchant for accuracy, the subsequent creedal statements and official proclamations of dogma solidified the "truth" of fourth-century Christianity for centuries to come.

The contemporary believer, thinking through these observations and recognizing the clear absence of what today one might call "fact," will no doubt feel some consternation. Who, one might wonder, was and is Jesus of Nazareth? How can we authentically connect with him in the context of our need for some historical grounding? Who is the God he witnessed to and made present to us? What ultimately is the meaning of redemption as somehow rooted in Jesus?

A certain reassurance can perhaps be gained if we try to approach the Gospels not so much as historical writings, but as vision statements originating in the Christ-centered experience of later Christianity. With Marcus Borg, we might understand them then as "the product of projecting later Christian convictions, grounded in the experience of Christ through the centuries as a living divine reality, back into the period of ministry itself."[7]

For us to be able to do this, however, it would seem that we clearly need to make a distinction between

• *Jesus of Nazareth, a human being,* who was not omnipresent or omnipotent and who could make mistakes, who shared, for example, the beliefs of his time about the world and its ultimate ending (which were subsequently found to be incorrect) and was, therefore, not omniscient, and

• *Jesus as the Christ,* who in and through the resurrection event (however one might understand it) became for his followers the manifestation of God and still, to this day, is seen through the eyes of faith as the presence and energy of the divine.

Putting it bluntly, Borg summarizes the necessary distinction as follows:

In short, the image of the historical Jesus as a divine or semi-divine being, who saw himself as the divine savior whose purpose was to die for the sins of the world, and whose message consisted of proclaiming that, is simply not *historically* true. Rather, it is the product of a blend produced by the early church — a blending of the *church's memory of Jesus* with the *church's beliefs about the risen Christ.* The former was seen through a window provided by the latter.[8]

And, as powerful as it may have been, the latter could not but find its articulation in the historical and cultural context of its time and use the words and concepts, metaphors and symbols it was familiar with to express its beliefs. Human beings function that way. It is the glory and the weakness of our finite condition. Expecting it to be different, wanting the totality of the past exactly as it was, encapsulated in total objectivity, belongs to a worldview no longer viable today. It is as much a "myth" (meaning here "fiction") as the "myth" it wants to avoid.

The quantum worldview emerging today suggests that the observer of any phenomenon is never a detached bystander but affects the reality being observed. The world, in other words, gives itself to us, appears to us, becomes real to us, according to our expectations of it, so that the observer is ever a part of the experiment, making objectivity impossible.[9] Some scientists use the term "omnijective" for this phenomenon to stress the interrelationship between the knower and the known, the observer and observed, the interpreter and what is being interpreted.

Applying this to the task of interpreting the Jesus experience Walter Wink says it well:

This means that there can be no question of an objective view of Jesus "as he really was." "Objective view" is itself an oxymoron; every view is subjective from a particular angle of vision. We always encounter the biblical text with interest. We always have a stake in our reading of it. We always have angles of vision, which can be helpful or harmful in interpreting texts. *"Historical writing does not treat reality; it treats the interpreter's relation to it...."* According to Hal Childs of the Guild for Psychological Studies...the past is not an object we can observe. It is an idea we have in the present about the past.[10]

Documents of the past, then, receive their meaning out of the present, and this will happen over and over again as the context of the time requires. Their value to us is in their effects on us in our time and culture and out of our present concerns, in the interplay and dialogue of past with present that provides us with the meaning and inspiration we need.[11]

Fullness of Humanity, Fullness of Divinity

What, then, is the Story we are "walking into"? Who is Jesus for us today, and how can we see him as real? I remember during my early years in religious life, when a friendly novice director told me one day with a radiant smile: "Remember, Barbara, Jesus was *so* human, he *had to be* divine." And that, perhaps, is where we need to start as we struggle with what seem to be two "realities" of Jesus and attempt to understand what "projecting later Christian convictions" back into the earthly existence of Jesus really means.

As I have tried, over the years, to take hold once again of a tangible connection, a meaningful presence to fill the

void that seemed to loom where in my youth the concrete-
ness of the historical Jesus had been, it came to me one
day that the power of projection is only as real its uncon-
sciousness.[12] And I started to ask myself what it was in
me that had drifted, or had been driven, below the surface
of my awareness; what it was in the subliminal regions of
my being — repressed or denied — that I was, therefore,
giving away, seeing in another, in Jesus of Nazareth, projecting outward instead of claiming; what it was in my
religion and in its church that we were giving away, so that
we would not have to face it, and claim it, and live it?

And the answer came clear as a bell: It was my, it was our
humanity — "divinized" in him through our projections,
unconscious in us and therefore unclaimed, made, in fact,
unreachable, somehow unattainable, as *his* divinity. It was
compassion beyond price and measure, unbounded mercy.
It was an acceptance and inclusion of all — saints and
sinners alike — the outcasts, the poor, women, yes, even
prostitutes. It was a rejection of oppression and oppressive systems of power, domination and everything needed
to keep control over others. It was a love for peace, and
passion, and tenderness. It was unconditional forgiveness.
It was the protection of children, of the helpless and vulnerable. It was a healing relationship to earth and all of
creation. It was the courage to stand for the vision of a
better world — the *reign of God* — even to the point of
death. At that moment, I came to know it all as part of
me, of what I was called to be in him who is the energy
field (as science might say), the light surrounding us as it
were, the "prescribed growth template" for us all, drawing

us into what we can be, our model, our fundamental paradigm, the primordial archetype for humanity, our truest destiny.

Truth beyond Objectivity

But (and here is an important shift) Jesus — the archetype of what humanity is and can be — was not, and can no longer be for us, "the omnipotent God in a man-suit," as Walter Wink puts it. He was and needs to be seen, instead, as truly "someone like us, who looked for God at the center of his life and called the world to join him."[13] He was someone also who sparked, and through the ages continues to spark, the fire of our yearning for authenticity and human integrity. The details of his onetime presence here on earth — of his life and what he said and did — are important for us, then, not primarily for their objective fact content, but for their significance *now,* for the present meaning they hold and the transformation they can effect in our time. It is here where we encounter "revelation" and the redeeming presence of the divine in the depth of the human.

"I don't know whether it happened," said the ancient storyteller, "but I know it is *true.*" And as such, it is important to hear.

What I am suggesting here in no way diminishes the importance of Jesus, or makes him any less "real" — insubstantial somehow, a figment of our imagination because the precise data about him are largely non-available, and we, therefore, "invented" him. There is something much bigger and more "real" at stake here and, indeed, something more "true" than facts in history as such. To touch its depth, however, we need to switch the "reality field" by which we are used to understanding the world. As I have said before, we need to see "truth" with different eyes: truth essentially as a presencing in the here and now, in the calling forth of our humanity today, what it can be now — not truth primarily as an account of what happened long ago.

The truth and redemptive power of the Jesus event for us lies in our empowerment today to let God's creative activity replace the staleness of egocentricity and greed, build a better world, and enhance God's reign. Jesus, who after his death was experienced as the Christ, is today "God with us" still, and that, primarily, by way of our humanization. Here the "Who am I?" question of "primary faith" (see chapter 2) and the "Who do you say I am?" question of scripture merge into one, as Christians continually, in every age, and out of the burning hunger of that age, reenter the energy field around his vision and are connected to, taken into, its truth *as their own.*

The Gospels are *true,* then, and their story is *real* — even as a collage of diverse perspectives[14] — because of the power they have to transform and touch, to call humanity to its deepest self, to "divinize":

- Simeon, the New Theologian, knew this in the tenth century, and so he could invite us to surrender and to let ourselves "receive the one who is opening to [us] so deeply. For if we genuinely love Him," Simeon promises, "we wake up *inside* Christ's body." We become Christified, if you will. The little shrub that we are becomes the adult plant we can be. Our hearts of stone are turned into flesh. "And everything that is hurt, everything that seemed to us dark, harsh, shameful, maimed, ugly, irreparably damaged, is in Him transformed and recognized as whole, as lovely, and *radiant in His light we awaken as the Beloved in every part of our body.*"

- The old monk in our story at the beginning of this chapter recognized it also, as he gazed into the pond, saw his reflection and the reflection of nature all around him, and began to understand what was meant by the "second coming": "When my presence in nature all around you and my presence beneath the surface of your skin is as real to you as my presence right now, when this awareness becomes second nature to you, *then* will I have returned for good." And so the old monk was finally able to *walk into the Story,* and the words at Jesus' baptism at last became "true" for him also: "You are my beloved son, in whom I am well pleased."

- Dorothy Stang knew it well. That is why she was dangerous, as were the martyrs of El Salvador and Liberia, as are the victims of abusive power everywhere who stand up against institutional domination, as are men and women throughout the ages who live the Christ vision that burns in the depths of our humanity and threatens all those who would deny it and remain inconsequential.

I Have Come to Cast Fire

So what is the fire that longs to be kindled in us (Luke 12:49)? What is the primary reason for the "Jesus event," as I like to call the entire field of transformative energy that includes

- both the man Jesus of Nazareth and what he said and did,

- and what we know of this man and have, through the centuries, come to see in him as the Christ?

What is the reason for Christianity and for the churches that claim him as their leader? What is, for me at least, and, I believe, for anyone who aches with "holy longing," the reason for our existence? The answer, I suggest, is simple and without pretense: *It is the reign of God*.

- We exist for it and for no other reason.

- The churches exist for it and for it alone.

- Christ Jesus lived for it and died for it.

It was what Wink calls his "original impulse." It was the drive behind his every word and deed. It was the power that impelled his message to take hold and spread throughout the world, to be spoken in new and diverse ways, to be enculturated and contextualized, interpreted and reinterpreted through the ages, for each age, even to this day.

◆ ◆ ◆

Perhaps one of the easiest ways to identify someone's passion or "original impulse" is to ask what she or he is willing to die for. Another way, less tangible perhaps and gentler, is to explore the how and what of someone's prayer. This too is true, I believe, of Jesus. I have in *Prayer and the Quest for Healing* reflected at length on the prayer Jesus taught. I reject the notion that it was ever meant to be a formula for recitation — a prayer to be said. In my own "projections" I see Jesus sharing his God-relation with his followers, sharing the intimacy that absorbed him and all that he did. The Abba of Jesus was his passion and fueled his rapture. The reign of Abba was the power behind his ministry, where he, in fact, translated his rapture into conviction and action even to the point of death.

My sense is that he wanted this for his followers, for us, wanted to kindle the fire, the Abba-centeredness and the compassion for all of humankind and all of creation that it brings with it. He wanted for us the surrender that comes with love, its freedom from domination and fear, its equality, its wholesomeness, its challenge, and its joy. He wanted it for us so that we too would spread the good news and help bring about transformation and wholeness for all.

So when his friends pleaded with him to teach them to pray, he tried to give them this vision and share his Abba-intimacy with them as a permeating attitude that would infuse all their praying and affect everything they did from then on, that would establish God's influence as all-pervasive in their lives, that would have them experience

the reign of God and give them the passion they needed
to live it and proclaim it:

> When you pray, allow the reality of God's uncondi-
> tional love to embrace you. See God, at all times, as
> you would a loving parent — as one who cherishes you
> unconditionally; as one for whom you are utterly im-
> portant; as one who knows your every need, shelters
> you in your vulnerability, and wishes you only good.
> Remember that God has birthed you into being; that
> God treasures you with infinite tenderness, listens to
> you with infinite patience, and reaches out to you at
> every moment of your existence. Dwell in this realiza-
> tion. Allow it to suffuse your very being. Know it in
> your innermost heart. Live it at your deepest core.[15]

Jesus' metaphor for his experience of the divine was
"Abba" — a child's expression for "father." For us, the
importance here does not lie in concretizing the male
characteristics or even the personalized, anthropomorphic
reality of God. It lies, rather, in what the experience
shared by Jesus should evoke in us and help bring about
in us. That, in fact, is what he stresses in the prayer he
teaches them as his very next concern: the establishment
of God's reign:

> If you do this [he seems to say], your life will be
> prayer. And you will be filled with the passionate long-
> ing that all of God's creatures will come to realize the
> presence of God in their lives; that Love's reign might
> be established on earth as, indeed, it exists among

the blessed who have passed into eternity already and throughout the universe.[16]

The "reign of God" as voiced through the prayer of Jesus clearly is a root metaphor of Christianity. It summarizes what we are about or ought to be about. It identifies what we believe Jesus lived for and died for. As I mentioned in a previous book, "root metaphors" are religious symbols that hold "an endless reservoir of depth and a perennial gift for drawing us forth."[17] And so we ask ourselves once again what we can understand by God's reign. To what are we drawn when we allow it to speak to us?

There is most likely no clearer response and bolder challenge to that question than Walter Wink's claim that God's reign is "God's Domination-Free Order." Jesus, in his living and his preaching, condemned all forms of domination:

- patriarchy and the oppression of women and children;
- the economic exploitation and impoverishment of entire classes of people;
- the family as chief instrument for the socialization of children into oppressive roles and values;
- hierarchical power arrangements that disadvantage the weak while benefiting the strong;
- the subversion of the law by the defenders of privilege;
- rules of purity that keep people separated;
- racial superiority and ethnocentrism;
- the entire sacrificial system with its belief in sacred violence.

Jesus proclaimed the reign of God...not only as
coming in the future, but as having already dawned in
his healings and exorcisms and his preaching of good
news to the poor. He created a new family, based
not on bloodlines, but on doing the will of God. He
espoused non-violence as a means for breaking the
spiral of violence without creating new forms of violence. He called people to repent of their collusion
in the Domination System and sought to heal them
from the various ways the system had dehumanized
them.[18]

This is what his radical love of God and humanity envi-
sioned and worked for. The God of Jesus is nonviolent
and all-inclusive. He not only preached this God, but lived
this God's vision — rooted, as it is, deep within the human
heart.

Called to One Table

I mentioned in chapter 3 ("Facing Our Reality") that faithfulness to this vision in its totality, especially through Jesus'
acceptance of all — modeled by a "shockingly" inclusive
table fellowship — was his life and, very likely, cost him
his life. And that, I believe, is why Eucharist, the meal of
Christian fellowship, is so necessary for Christianity even
to this day and perhaps especially today.

Bland ritualism and the pedantic concern to maintain it
are not enough here, however. Eucharist calls us to con-
science, and if it does not, it betrays Jesus Christ and the

dangerous memory we were baptized to embrace. Table fellowship in the earliest Christian communities was what the table fellowship of Jesus had been throughout his time of ministry. It marked the community gathered in memory of the one who was "a friend of tax collectors and sinners," and was maligned as "a glutton and drunkard" by those who could not stomach such inclusion (Matt. 11:16–19). We have every reason to believe that the meal practice of the earliest Christians "was something out of the ordinary" and not merely a result of their Jewish heritage (the Passover, for example, or Qumran communal meals). It pointed primarily to their *identity*, as they continued "a regular practice of the ministry of Jesus."[19]

Furthermore, the emphasis for the early followers of Jesus was on the meal, specifically, not on the theology or ritual associated with it, which came much later, as Norman Perrin explains:

> The existence of such different theological emphases as those connected with the "Lord's Supper" in the New Testament (1 Cor. 11) is an indication that the occasion has called forth the theologies, not the theologies the occasion. The practice of early Christian communal meals existed before there was a specific Christian theology to give it meaning. We may not argue that the meals are an echo of the "last supper" held by Jesus with his disciples during the Passion. . . . All our evidence indicates that the kind of theological emphasis associated with the "last supper" in the gospels was by no means the major emphasis in early

Christian communal meals from the very beginning, as it would have been if this had been the occasion for them.[20]

My reflections here on the significance of the meal for the followers of Jesus do not imply, of course, that later theological developments are therefore not important and should be disregarded. It is rather out of a serious concern for what appears to me as a loss of emphasis on, and possibly a lack of understanding of, the primary intent of Jesus and the identity of his original followers. Perrin in his study goes to considerable lengths to identify what might, in fact, be original behaviors and sayings of Jesus. His table fellowship with both religious and social outcasts seems to be primary here. We are, says Perrin, justified therefore to claim it "as the central feature of the ministry of Jesus: an anticipatory sitting at table in the Kingdom of God and a very real celebration of present joy and challenge."[21]

And it is the "challenge" that we cannot allow ourselves to forget or ignore in the religious climate of today. I mentioned this in chapter 3, but it bears repeating here, that to use Christian table fellowship — the Eucharist — as a mark of the official acceptance of an individual, of approval of his or her moral perspective or social and political stance, to use one's official position, in other words, to include or exclude at will those with whom one agrees or disagrees, is a shameful abuse of power — the very same abuse that Jesus objected to and that was ultimately used to hand him over to his crucifiers. It flies in the face of the original Jesus vision of community as inclusive and universal,[22] where people "will come from east and west, and north and south, and sit at table in the kingdom of God" (Luke 13:29). Their official membership in the church, or their proper belief, their sexual orientation, their position on abortion, their view of women's right to ordination, their "worthiness" are not the issue.

What defies my understanding is how we have come to accept clearly "unchristian" norms as standard ecclesial practice today and have, in fact, and with unblinking self-righteousness, enforced them in our churches. "The covenant of the Eucharist, the New Covenant in Christ Jesus, is the commitment, even to the point of death, to God's cause — to the holiness, health, and wholesomeness that blossoms in a society of equals where all are welcome and all are fed around the table of God's justice."[23]

For unto Us a Child Is Born

On a symbolic level, it would seem that right from the beginning of his life Jesus was meant to witness to God's preferential option for the poor and outcasts of society. As I have often suggested in my retreats, Christmas, contrary to what is frequently claimed, is really a feast for grown-ups and would challenge us to the core, if we could understand its message that way.

It is true that over the years commercialization has served to deplete the feast of Christ's birth of its scriptural significance, and the cribs beneath the altar, the red and green and gold in all their splendor have tended to divert our attention from the reality of the story — whether it actually happened or not. What the writers of Matthew and Luke "projected" into the birth of Jesus has nothing to do with ringing bells, sweet carols, and poinsettias, but points, once again, to the "original impulse" we have been reflecting on.

Jesus, as the story tells it, was born in a cave — not a friendly place. It was cold, dirty, and devoid of all human comforts. There was no room for his parents in the inn, I suggest, because they had no means to pay. (In a contemporary reading of this story we could say, without prejudice, that had they presented payment, there would have been room. The levy break in New Orleans is America's litmus test for this — just ask who got out and when, and who was left behind and why.) What welcomed the "Son of Man" to this earth was misery. Shepherds — the lowest of the low — were told of his birth and came to see. Foreigners, wise Gentiles from various far places, came later to pay him homage with gifts that foretold his mission and his dying.

The emergence of God through the birth of Jesus, therefore, as Luke portrays it, is about God's being for the outcast and the stranger we ignore, for the unimportant — those without money. This is so, not because God likes oppression and misery, but because the oppressed and poor are deprived of so much of what God wants for them. The reign of God is for the whole world, for all of God's creation — a place of wholeness, health, and happiness for all. Instead, Mary and Joseph were hungry and cold and scared and dirty, probably discouraged, and certainly tired, and that is what Christmas shows us if we would but see.

Christmas, looked at through adult eyes, challenges us to the core. Poverty and displacement and being refugees are terrible plights. But God in Jesus, so our story tells it, chose visibility *there*. And Jesus, throughout his life of ministry, continues to direct our attention *there*. The symbols of our Story are stark and very direct: From the very beginning until his death on the cross — crucified, an outcast between two outcasts — and even after his resurrection,[24] Jesus and the God he came to proclaim are about transforming the structures of oppression, about being *there* and working from the inside out. Passion for God's reign commits us to the same — to building a world where the poor and their children do not need to find refuge in caves and stables, on street corners, under bridges and, yes, in convention centers, but will have food and shelter and a chance in life.

Poverty and oppression are the results of an "order of domination," as Wink calls it, and God needs us to be about changing that. That is what it means to be about God's reign. That is what is meant by "God's ongoing creation." That too is what is meant by redemption.

Because We Believe

In chapter 1, I wondered whether the world was, in fact, a better place because we believe. The reflection above sets the stage for an answer. The "better place" — God's reign — is what we believe Jesus came to establish. He described it in the Beatitudes. Its tools are the works of mercy, and we, whether we knew it or not, were baptized into its coming and are committed by the fullness of the humanity deep within us to bring it about. There are no pretensions or idealistic fantasies here. The Christian agenda is clear. It is our destiny and our judgment.

Chapter 5 exposed us to our radical interconnectedness and the amazing powers that lie within us and are manifest in the whole universe as an expression of the divine. The worldview we are encountering in our day does not allow us to retreat to the safety of separatism and individualism any longer. The healing we work heals us also. The harm and selfishness we wreak on others eventually breaks us down as well.

It is not possible any longer to hide behind a redemptive act performed, "once and for all," by the saving death of Christ, atoning for our sins. There is no finality in a constantly evolving and changing cosmos, and, though the "for all" is guaranteed to our every act and every thought by virtue of our interconnectedness, the "once" disappears in the constant challenge to transform and heal what still longs for the redemptive power of love and awaits our free "yes." Teresa of Avila was right: "Christ has no body now but yours."

There can be a certain escapism in one's association with a church whose leadership sees itself as "dispensing" the sacraments and, most shocking of all, "dispensing" the Body of Christ, "bringing him down from heaven" into the assembly gathered for that moment and waiting to receive him. Passivity can creep into one's life when "Father" does

it all. We are "fed" each week as long as we come to fulfill
our Sunday obligations. The one who "feeds" can easily
get a false sense of power that he claims as his by virtue of
being *in persona Christi*. I remember a young cleric boast-
ing to me at a faculty gathering about his generosity that
morning when he had consented to use inclusive language
at Mass to make the women who were present feel good.
I told him, perhaps not as kindly as I could have, that it
wasn't his Mass. That it was the Eucharist of the assembly at which he was presiding, and that he had no business
excluding anyone if in fact he accepted the teachings of
Jesus. He was dumbfounded.

What can be forgotten so easily when we adopt this kind
of attitude is the *reason* for our gathering — that it is, in
fact, a gathering of the very Body that we think is "being
dispensed to us," a Body that *we are in him*. It is a meal
that celebrates the Presence experienced in the Memory —
the dangerous Memory — of the one who gave his life out
of love so that all would become one in that love, so that
we too would love one another and commit that love to all
humanity, all of creation and, in so doing, become whole.

I am returning here to the Augustinian (as different from
the Ambrosian) interpretation of Eucharist "that stressed
the dynamic, symbolic unifying power of the sacrament,
incorporating all into the mystical body of Christ."[25] For
Augustine the power of the Eucharist lies in the assembly's
unity with each other and with God. "It is the faithful re-
cipients who make the body of Christ present by *becoming*
it."[26] In his *Interpreting John's Gospel* 27.6, Augustine em-
phasizes: "We abide in him when we are his members, and

he abides in us when we are his temple. And for us to become his members, unity must bind us to each other." Augustine, as well as Ignatius of Antioch some two centuries earlier, "would never have thought that reverence to the Eucharist involved removing its mystery from the midst of the believers. They would not have fenced off the altar, since the people *were* the altar, just as they were the bread lying on it."[27] Sending some of the bread used for the Eucharistic meal to other communities was a common practice in Augustine's time, a sign of their oneness in Christ.[28]

Membership in a community gathered in Christ's name is not meant to be passive and provide an escape from mutual responsibility. We will destroy ourselves, and all we were meant to be, that way. Perhaps no one has said this quite as bluntly as did Richard Rohr in his "Lenten Series" for the *National Catholic Reporter* (February 15, 2002):

> I don't know why we are satisfied with such utter passivity in most Catholic parishes. Are we actually happy to be kept as subservient little children who ask for nothing and give little in return? ... It is bad enough that we priests are content with such overwhelming passivity, but sometimes I think we actually prefer it. It keeps us in control, with no one asking hard questions, and actually decreases the workload. Participatory faith community is a lot of extra work and meetings and people. Church as liminal space would require solid biblical preaching, contemplative Eucharists, and a cadre of female and male spiritual

directors and ministries. Instead, we are reasserting the role and centrality of the priest like never before. Even the deacons must kneel. Siege mentality, I guess. The quiet noncooperation and passivity will only increase, I promise you. Bishops, please listen.[29]

Eucharist, and the energy unleashed for the sake of justice, is an explosive moment that sends vibrations throughout the universe and, therefore, through us as well who are, each one of us, the center of that universe. It cannot be a "from-the-outside-in" event, therefore, and retain the power of Christian table fellowship, of a community of equals gathered to bring about God's reign. The Jesus of the Gospels did not want passivity parading as reverence from those gathered with him at table. The meal marked their *personal* as well as their *communal* commitment to transformation. It was, as I said above, their very symbol of Christian identity. They became one around a common vision and a common goal. I believe we, today, are meant to be about that same unity. Lack of involvement belies this and belies the redemptive work to which we are all called.

Homecoming

Within this context it becomes clear that we walk the road of redemption, each one of us every day, for ourselves as well as for each other. We reflected on this in chapter 3 as the "Grand Option" to give ourselves up for the sake of all. We saw it there as our *yes* to the building of authentic community, and as the next step in evolution. I mention it here only to emphasize the "movement away," which this implies, from the traditional concept of an offended deity demanding restitution for a sin committed by the first man, Adam. We were said to have inherited this sin through the sexual pleasure of our parents during intercourse.[30]

For many of us, this "movement away" is difficult, largely because what we have accepted for so long has been understood as the life-blood of Christianity. It is important, therefore, to stress that we are here doing away neither with the reality of sin, nor with the need for redemption and healing. Both are dimensions of human existence that have cried for an understanding since the beginning of consciousness. Both find valiant attempts at explanations in every religion I can think of.

Within the worldview that is emerging in our time, it is becoming more and more evident, however, that the Christian explanation of an offended Father God choosing his Son to be crucified in expiation for our sin can no longer evoke a mature, contemporary faith response. It spoke to an ancient sacrificial cult orientation whose context is no longer ours. In later times, it also spoke to the mediaeval feudal structure of governance discussed in chapter 3. It was embellished and given a logical fit probably most clearly by Anselm of Canterbury (1033–1109). The system of the time (as was discussed in "Structures of Domination") had clear categories of power and submission, with laws of reward and punishment seen necessary for its survival. Punishment was demanded as restitution for crimes and seen as restoring (in the sense of such synonyms as "restitution," "repayment," "recompense") the hierarchical order that had been violated by the offense.

Creation as a whole was understood in a similar fashion. When the head of creation, Adam, sinned, the cosmic order was damaged and, along with us who were part of it, needed to be "restored." The offense against God, however, could not be wiped away by a mere human. Atonement demanded a higher order of restitution. Hence, God "so loved the world" as to send his Son to atone for Adam's sin and reestablish the divine order in the universe.

In chapter 1 ("Dangerous Memories") I wondered why so many believers in Christ seemingly are so afraid of his freedom; why explorations into other possibilities of faith interpretation, into more contemporary reflections on the events we call salvation history, are so often treated with scorn. Clearly the fear of disagreement with the teaching authority of the church is one explanation — one wonders about the sense of it all, but does not dare ask. The succeeding chapters have, hopefully, explored the necessity of returning to a primordial faith response (a personal *yes* to the Mystery and to depth meaning) on the part of every adult believer. I suggested that this is particularly important in the light of the emerging worldview of our time, which no longer can sustain many of the explanations based on dualism and the hierarchism it supported. Fundamental depravity due to sin and the evil of matter and the body simply do not fit into contemporary cosmology filled with the wonder and overwhelming awe before the majesty of the universe.

What is the Story we are "walking into"? Who is Jesus for us today, and how can we see him as real?

Nevertheless, sin is real, and so is our need to address it in ourselves and in the structures of oppression that foster it. That the world and the church need redemption is not disputed in these pages. The emphasis, however, is on the journey each of us is called to embrace:

- to promote the vision of God's reign and foster a world community of mutual support and the empowerment of all;

- to be the light that we are in the midst of the darkness that still prevails both in ourselves and in the world.

Christians believe that this journey was modeled for us by Jesus — both as he was while on earth and as the Spirit has led us to understand him in the centuries that followed his earthly existence even to this day.

Revelation for us, then, as well as redemption, are ongoing experiences in which we are intimately involved. Our maturity and our time in history convince us that we cannot "pass the buck" any longer and wait passively for someone to tell us what it is now proper to believe or to do. We are connected to each other and to God, and as such we are responsible for the world we live in.

Thoughts and Questions for Meditation

What are your thoughts concerning the following selections from chapter 6?

1. "Walking into the Story," means surrendering to its deepest truth. It means accepting it as our charter,

our reality, whose gathering point and healing symbol for all Christians is ever Christ Jesus, "leading us with relentless love into conversion: at-onement with our inmost being and through this, mysteriously, with the universe as well."

2. What are your reactions to the point made in the section "Courage to Face the Unknown" (page 149)? How do you react to the suggestion that one approach the Gospels not so much as historical writings in themselves, but as vision statements originating in the Christ-centered experience of later Christianity, as the product of projecting later Christian convictions, grounded in the experience of Christ through the centuries as a living divine reality, back into the period of ministry itself?

3. The image of the historical Jesus as a divine or semi-divine being, who saw himself as the divine savior whose purpose was to die for the sins of the world, and whose message consisted of proclaiming that, is simply not *historically* true. Rather, it is the product of a blend produced by the early church — a blending of the *the church's memory of Jesus* with the *church's beliefs about the risen Christ.* The former was seen through a window provided by the latter. And, as powerful as it may have been, the latter could not but find its articulation in the historical and cultural context of its time, and use the words and concepts, metaphors and symbols it was familiar with to express its beliefs. Human beings function that way. It is the

glory and the weakness of our finite condition. Expecting it to be different, wanting the totality of the past exactly as it was, encapsulated in total objectivity, belongs to a worldview no longer viable today. It is as much a "myth" (meaning here "fiction") as the "myth" it wants to avoid.

4. What are your thoughts on the invitation to claim and retrieve our "projections" — those aspects of our humanity that have drifted or have been driven below the surface of our awareness, that we are giving away and "seeing" in a divine being but not in ourselves so that we do not have to face them or take hold of them and live them (see "Fullness of Humanity, Fullness of Divinity," page 155)?

5. But (and here is an important shift) Jesus — the archetype of what humanity is and can be — was not, and can no longer be for us, "the omnipotent God in a man-suit," as Walter Wink puts it. He was and needs to be seen, instead, as truly "someone like us, who looked for God at the center of his life and called the world to join him." He was someone also who sparked, and through the ages continues to spark, the fire of our yearning for authenticity and human integrity. The details of his one time presence here on earth — of his life and what he said and did — are important for us, then, not primarily for their objective fact content, but for their significance now, for the present meaning they hold and the transformation they can effect in our time. It is here where we encounter "revelation"

and the redeeming presence of the divine in the depth of the human. "I don't know whether it happened," said the ancient storyteller, "but I know it is *true*." And as such, it is important to hear.

6. The truth and redemptive power of the Jesus event for us lies in our empowerment today to let God's creative activity replace the staleness of egocentricity and greed, build a better world, and enhance God's reign. Jesus, who after his death was experienced as the Christ, is today "God with us" still, and that, primarily, by way of our humanization. Here the "Who am I?" question of "primary faith" (see chapter 2) and the "Who do you say I am?" question of scripture merge into one, as Christians continually, in every age, and out of the burning hunger of that age, reenter the energy field around his vision and are connected to, taken into, its truth *as their own*. The Gospels are *true*, then, and their story is *real* — even as a collage of diverse perspectives — because of the power they have to transform and touch, to call humanity to its deepest self, to "divinize."

7. Perhaps one of the easiest ways to identify someone's passion or "original impulse" is to ask what she or he is willing to die for. Another way, less tangible perhaps and gentler, is to explore the how and what of someone's prayer. This too is true, I believe, of Jesus. I have in *Prayer and the Quest for Healing* reflected at length on the prayer Jesus taught. I reject the notion that it was ever meant to be a formula for recitation — a

prayer to be said. In my own "projections" I see Jesus sharing his God-relation with his followers, sharing the intimacy that absorbed him and all that he did. The Abba of Jesus was his passion and fueled his rapture. The reign of Abba was the power behind his ministry, where he, in fact, translated his rapture into conviction and action even to the point of death.

8. What is your response to Walter Wink's description of the "reign of God" as "God's Domination-Free Order"? See his enumeration of "forms of domination" in "I Have Come to Cast Fire" (page 163).

9. Reflect and respond to Jesus' "shockingly" inclusive table fellowship that "was his life and, very likely, cost him his life" (see "Called to One Table," page 164). My reflections here on the significance of the meal for the followers of Jesus do not imply, of course, that later theological developments are, therefore, not important and should be disregarded. It is rather out of a serious concern for what appears to me as a loss of emphasis on, and possibly a lack of understanding of, the primary intent of Jesus and the identity of his original followers. Perrin in his study goes to considerable lengths to identify what might, in fact, be original behaviors and sayings of Jesus. His table fellowship with both religious and social outcasts seems to be primary here. We are, says Perrin, justified, therefore, to claim it "as the central feature of the ministry of Jesus: an anticipatory sitting at table in the Kingdom of God and a very real celebration of present joy and challenge."

10. To use Christian table fellowship — the Eucharist — as a mark of the official acceptance of an individual, of approval of his or her moral perspective or social and political stance; to use one's official position, in other words, to include or exclude at will those with whom one agrees or disagrees, is a shameful abuse of power — the very same abuse that Jesus objected to and that was ultimately used to hand him over to his crucifiers. It flies in the face of the original Jesus vision of community as inclusive and universal, where people "will come from east and west, and north and south, and sit at table in the kingdom of God" (Luke 13:29). Their official membership in the church, their proper belief, their sexual orientation, their position on abortion, their view of women's right to ordination, their "worthiness" are not the issue.

11. The emergence of God through the birth of Jesus, therefore, as Matthew and Luke portray it, is about God's being for the outcast and the stranger we ignore, for the unimportant — those without money. This is so, not because God likes oppression and misery, but because the oppressed and poor are deprived of so much of what God wants for them. The reign of God is for the whole world, for all of God's creation — a place of wholeness, health, and happiness for all. Instead, Mary and Joseph were hungry and cold and scared and dirty, probably discouraged, and certainly tired, and that is what Christmas shows us if we would but see. Christmas, looked at through adult

eyes, challenges us to the core. Poverty and displacement and being refugees are terrible plights. But God in Jesus, so our story tells it, chose visibility *there*.

12. Poverty and oppression are the results of an "order of domination," as Wink calls it, and God needs us to be about changing that. That is what it means to be about God's reign. That is what is meant by "God's ongoing creation." That too is what is meant by redemption. It is not possible any longer to hide behind a redemptive act performed, "once and for all," by the saving death of Christ, atoning for our sins. There is no finality in a constantly evolving and changing cosmos, and, though the "for all" is guaranteed to our every act and every thought by virtue of our interconnectedness, the "once" disappears in the constant challenge to transform and heal what still longs for the redemptive power of love and awaits our free "yes." Teresa of Avila was right: "Christ has no body now but yours."

13. Eucharist, and the energy unleashed for the sake of justice, is an explosive moment that sends vibrations throughout the universe and, therefore, through us as well who are, each one of us, the center of that universe. It cannot be a "from-the-outside-in" event, therefore, and retain the power of Christian table fellowship, of a community of equals gathered to bring about God's reign. The Jesus of the Gospels did not want passivity parading as reverence from those gathered with him at table. The meal marked their personal

as well as their communal commitment to transformation. It was their very symbol of Christian identity. They became one around a common vision and a common goal. I believe we, today, are meant to be about that same unity. Lack of involvement belies this and belies the redemptive work to which we are all called.

14. In the section "Homecoming" (page 173) a rethinking of the traditional understanding of redemption invites some serious reflection. What is your response? How have you come to see sin and revelation in the reading of this book?

Notes

1. Introduction

1. See Christoph Schönborn, "Finding Design in Nature," *New York Times,* July 7, 2005; legal positions on this issue as it relates to education abound throughout the United States.

2. David Steindl-Rast, "Solving The God Problem," *Spirituality and Health* 8, no. 3 (May–June 2005): 57.

3. For a more detailed discussion of this Arthurian tale see Barbara Fiand, *Wrestling with God: Religious Life in Search of Its Soul* (New York: Crossroad, 1996), 3–9.

4. Ibid., 8.

5. For a detailed discussion of this phenomenon, especially in the lives of women, see Miriam Therese Winter, Adair Lummis, and Allison Stokes, *Defecting in Place: Women Claiming Responsibility for Their Own Lives* (New York: Crossroad, 1994).

2. Primordial Faith

1. Barbara Fiand, *Embraced by Compassion: On Human Longing and Divine Response* (New York: Crossroad, 1993), 29.

2. Karl Rahner, cited in Ibid.

3. Ibid.

4. For an interesting reflection on this see Karen Armstrong, *A Short History of Myth* (New York: Canongate, 2005), chapters 1, 2.

5. Ibid.

6. Diarmuid Ó Murchú, *Reclaiming Spirituality: A New Spiritual Framework for Today's World* (New York: Crossroad, 1998), vii.

7. Ibid.

8. Anne Carr, "On Feminist Spirituality," in *Women's Spirituality: Resources for Christian Development,* ed. Joan Wolski Conn
(New York: Paulist, 1986), 49.

9. Ibid., 50.

10. Ibid.

11. Petru Dumitriu, *To the Unknown God,* trans. James Kirkup
(New York: Seabury Press, 1982), 56.

12. Jack Nelson-Pallmeyer, *War Against the Poor: Low-Intensity
Conflict and Christian Faith* (Maryknoll, N.Y.: Orbis Books,
1990), 75.

3. Situating Ourselves

1. Beatrice Bruteau, *The Grand Option: Personal Transformation and a New Creation* (Notre Dame, Ind.: University of Notre
Dame Press, 2001), 1–2.

2. Ibid.

3. Ibid., 2.

4. Ibid., 3.

5. Donald Nichol, *Holiness* (New York: Seabury Press, 1981),
chapter 3.

6. Bruteau, *The Grand Option,* 6.

7. Ibid., 7.

8. Elisabeth Schüssler Fiorenza, *In Memory of Her* (New York:
Crossroad, 1984), 135; emphasis added.

9. Ibid., 135–36; emphasis added.

10. Norman Perrin, *Rediscovering the Teaching of Jesus* (New
York: Harper & Row, 1967), 103.

11. Mary T. Malone, *Women and Christianity: The First Thousand Years,* vol. 1 (Maryknoll, N.Y.: Orbis, 2001), 65.

12. Ibid., 62.

13. It is my sense that the education of women that ultimately
allowed them to see themselves in a better light, in spite of the
belittlement that continued to come their way from organized
religion, was a major factor in their emancipation. That education was initiated, in great part, by the "service" communities of
women religious, which were founded precisely for that purpose.

In my lectures to religious congregations of women through-out the world (few of which would openly consider themselves "feminist"), I mention this as a valid reason for justified cele-bration and honest pride. For an interesting study on the work and struggle of women's congregations dedicated to this task see Mary T. Malone, *Women and Christianity*, vol. 3 (Maryknoll, N.Y.: Orbis, 2003), chapters 4 and 5.

14. "Orthodox" as opposed to "heretical." The latter included all those who, though they understood themselves as follow-ers of Christ, did not interpret things in what was perceived to be the "correct" way. The claim of orthodoxy was direct lineage of thought from the apostles. Scholars today generally hold that what came to be known as orthodox Christianity (Bart Ehrman's "proto-orthodoxy") was "simply one of many com-peting interpretations of Christianity in the early church. It was neither a *self-evident* interpretation nor an *original apostolic* view. The apostles, for example, did not teach the Nicene Creed or anything like it. Indeed, as far as we can trace it, Christianity was remarkably varied in its theological expression" (Bart D. Ehrman, *Lost Christianities: The Battle for Scripture and the Faiths We Never Knew* [New York: Oxford University Press, 2003], 176; emphasis added). What in our religious interpretations today many of us innocently believe dates back to Jesus himself really developed as the view that "won out" — never smoothly and always in the face of much diversity — during the first four centuries.

15. Ehrman, *Lost Christianities*, 174. For a detailed discussion on the battle for unity, the victory of "proto-orthodoxy," and the rewriting of history see the introduction and chapters 8, 11, and 12.

16. Ibid., 255–56.

17. Ibid., 256.

18. Ibid., 250.

19. Donald Cozzens, *Faith That Dares to Speak* (Collegeville, Minn.: Liturgical Press, 2004), 12–13.

20. Ibid., 13; emphasis added.

21. The term "curia" is derived from the ancient senate house at Rome. Since 1840 it refers to "the Papal court including all its authorities and functionaries" (*Oxford Universal Dictionary on Historical Principles*). I use the word "ruling" advisedly, since, in spite of declarations of unchanging and eternal teachings that have on occasion been ascribed highhandedly to mere curial opinions, centuries (as in Galileo's case) and sometimes merely a change in pope (as in the case of Teilhard de Chardin) can bring about eventual changes in perspective — though in both examples mentioned here, those silenced were by then dead.

22. Cozzens, *Faith That Dares to Speak,* 13–14.

23. Ibid., 9.

4. Expanding Our Horizons

1. Paula D'Arcy, *A New Set of Eyes: Encountering the Hidden God* (New York: Crossroad, 2002), 13, 14.

2. Ibid., 15.

3. Ibid.

4. For a more detailed discussion on Job as a symbol for our time, see my book *Prayer and the Quest for Healing: Our Personal Transformation and Cosmic Responsibility* (New York: Crossroad, 1999), chapter 13. I owe this discussion in large part to Camilla Burns's public lecture on Job given at Loyola University Chicago, November 6, 1998.

5. For detailed discussion on "Forgotten Papal Statements, and How They Have Changed through the Centuries," see Maureen Fiedler and Linda Rabbin, eds., *Rome Has Spoken* (New York: Crossroad, 1998). It becomes obvious to the reader of these pages that Catholicism too is contextual — a human response to the Mystery — and subject to change, in spite of protestations to the contrary. See also Garry Wills, *Papal Sin: Structures of Deceit* (New York: Doubleday, 2000). Wills here identifies the obfuscation and denial of ecclesial "mistakes" and "misrepresentations" of scripture as well as of tradition.

6. Karen Armstrong, *A Short History of Myth* (New York: Canongate, 2005), 24.

7. Ibid., 23.

8. For an interesting and easily read discussion of Einstein's discovery see Brian Swimme, *The Hidden Heart of the Cosmos* (Maryknoll, N.Y.: Orbis), chapters 9, 10, and 11.

9. D'Arcy, *A New Set of Eyes,* 15.

10. Ibid.

11. Ibid., 16; emphasis added.

12. Barbara Fiand, *In the Stillness You Will Know: Exploring the Paths of Our Ancient Belonging* (New York: Crossroad, 2002), 114.

13. Rudolf Otto, *The Idea of the Holy,* trans. John W. Harvey (New York: Oxford University Press, 1970), 26.

14. Ibid., 27.

15. For further discussion on the hologram, see my book *In the Stillness You Will Know,* especially chapter 3, p. 90. For the reader's convenience the explanation found there is as follows: "A holograph is perhaps most easily understood as a three-dimensional picture obtained via a split laser beam. While the first beam is bounced off the desired object, the other beam is allowed to collide with the reflected light causing what is called an interference pattern. When this is recorded on film and yet another laser beam made to shine through this film, a three-dimensional picture of the original object is the result. What is remarkable and significant in a hologram is the fact that, unlike an ordinary photograph which, if cut into a number of pieces, will yield only partial images of the whole for each piece, the cut-up pieces of the holograph will each yield the entire three-dimensional picture, thus illustrating that, indeed, the whole is contained in each of its parts." Scientists today are becoming ever more convinced that the universe as a whole needs to be understood as a holographic whole. For more detail see also Michael Talbot, *The Holographic Universe* (New York: Harper Perennial, 1991).

16. Danah Zohar, *The Quantum Self: Human Nature and Consciousness Defined by the New Physics* (New York: Quill/William Morrow, 1990), 36–37.

17. Fiand, *In the Stillness You Will Know,* 91.

18. The physics that provides us with the post-mechanistic worldview that is emerging today frequently does so in highly abstract mathematical formulae that only later are proved through experiment. Understanding the intricacies of this physics is clearly not our goal here. The view offered us by physics, however, is amazingly close to the experiences of mystics throughout the ages and truly relevant for retrieving a primary faith experience and the spirituality that supports it.

19. *Catechism of the Catholic Church* (New York: Paulist Press, 1994), no. 659.

20. Ibid., no. 966.

5. An Invitation to Wonder

1. Jane Clark, "Contemplating Nature, with Arthur Zajonc," *Noetic Sciences Review* no. 23 (Autumn 1992): 8. See online at *www.noetic.org/publications/review/issue 23/r23_Clark.html*

2. Ibid.

3. Ibid., 7.

4. Ibid., 9.

5. Fritjof Capra, *The Turning Point: Science, Society and the Rising Culture* (New York: Simon and Schuster, 1982), 15.

6. The story was told by Helen Roseveare, a missionary doctor from England, and appears in her book *Living Faith* (London: Hodder & Stoughton, 1988). It also appears on numerous Web sites, e.g., *www.truthorfiction.com/rumors/h/hotwaterbottle.htm.*

7. For an interesting discussion of scientific experiments sponsored at Stanford and Princeton Universities that explore the human capacity to transcend time and space — "non-locality" and "non-temporality" — see Lynne McTaggart, *The Field: The Quest for the Secret Force of the Universe* (New York: Quill, 2003), chapter 9. These studies, McTaggart observes: "began to suggest that at a more fundamental level of existence, there is no space or time, no obvious cause and effect — of something hitting something else and causing an event over time and space.

Newtonian ideas of an absolute time and space or even Einstein's view of a relative space-time are replaced by a truer picture — that the universe exists in some vast 'here' where here represents all points of space and time at a single instant. If subatomic particles can interact across all space and time, then so might the larger matter they compose. In the quantum world of 'The Field,' a subatomic world of pure potential, life exists as *one enormous present.* 'Take *time* out of it,' Robert Jahn was fond of saying, 'and it all makes sense'" (emphasis added). See also *www.stephenaschwartz.com* and *www.schwartzreport.net.* Nonlocality and our capacity to transcend distance have been the subject of intense study for years by the Central Intelligence Agency, which has released nearly twelve thousand documents (ninety thousand pages) detailing the U.S. government's research into "Remote Viewing" for purposes, among other things, of espionage. See *www.rviewer.com/SGArchive.html.*

8. See Eckhart Tolle, *The Power of Now* (Novato, Calif.: New World Library, 1999), 27–28, 46–51.

9. Danah Zohar, *The Quantum Self: Human Nature and Consciousness Defined by the New Physics* (New York: Quill/William Morrow, 1990), 34.

10. Ibid., 58.

11. Ibid.

12. Einstein cited by Marilyn Ferguson, *The Brain Revolution: The Frontiers of Mind Research* (New York: Bantam Books, 1975), 352.

13. McTaggart, *The Field,* 21.

14. Zohar, *The Quantum Self,* 236.

15. McTaggart, *The Field,* 24.

16. Brian Swimme, *The Hidden Heart of the Cosmos: Humanity and the New Story* (Maryknoll, N.Y.: Orbis, 1996), 93, 97, 100.

17. Ferguson, *The Brain Revolution,* 351. See also Franci Prowse with Cleve Backster, "Exploring a Sentient World," *Shift: At the Frontiers of Consciousness,* no. 11 (June–August 2006):20–23.

18. Ferguson, *The Brain Revolution,* 351–52.

19. Michael Talbot, *Mysticism and the New Physics* (London: Arkana, 1993), 93. Talbot here references J. R Smythies, *Analysis of Perception* (New York: Humanities, 1956).

20. Piaget as discussed in Talbot, *Mysticism and the New Physics,* 93.

21. Sheila Ostrander and Lynn Schroeder, *Psychic Discoveries behind the Iron Curtain* (New York: Bantam Books, 1970), 33–34.

22. Agnes Sanford, *The Healing Light* (Plainfield, N.J.: Logos International, 1972), 53–54.

23. I received this letter via a multiple-address e-mail, but I suspect it originated as one of her "Newsletters" (see online at *www.drnorthrup.com/newsletter.php*).

24. McTaggart, *The Field,* 190. Christiane Northrup cites several experiments in her letter as well: "When a critical mass of individuals (1 percent of the population) was brought together to practice Transcendental Meditation in various areas of the world, for example, there was a measurable decrease in the number of violent crimes, suicides, terrorist attacks, and even international conflicts worldwide." See David Orme-Johnson et al., "International Peace Project in the Middle East: The Effect of the Maharishi Technology on the Unified Field," *Journal of Conflict Resolution* 32, no. 4 (1988): 776–812.

25. Paul Pearsall, Ph.D., *The Heart's Code: Tapping the Wisdom and Power of Our Heart Energy* (New York: Broadway Books, 1999), 7.

26. McTaggart, *The Field,* 94

27. Deepak Chopra, M.D., *Quantum Healing: Exploring the Frontiers of Mind/Body Medicine* (New York: Bantam Books, 1990), 146.

28. Christian Wertenbaker, "The Eye of the Beholder: Paradoxes of the Visible Universe," *Parabola* 26, no. 2 (May 2001): 51.

29. For a discussion on the invisibility of light except for its power to illuminate objects, see Arthur Zajonc, *Catching*

the Light: The Entwined History of Light and Mind (New York: Oxford University Press, 1993), 2–3.

30. Ibid., 327. The name scientists give to this shimmering, special kind of light is: "zero point energy of the vacuum."

31. McTaggart, *The Field*, 94.

32. Wertenbaker, "The Eye of the Beholder," 51; emphasis added.

33. Barbara Fiand, *In the Stillness You Will Know: Exploring the Paths of Our Ancient Belonging* (New York: Crossroad, 2002), 25.

34. Richard Gerber, M.D., *Vibrational Medicine: The #1 Handbook of Subtle-Energy Therapies,* 3rd ed. (Rochester, Vt.: Bear & Company, 2001), 59.

35. Zajonc, *Catching the Light:,* 314–15.

36. Jacques Lusseyran, *And There Was Light*, trans., Elizabeth R. Cameron (New York: Parabola Books, 1998), 16–17.

37. Ibid., 17.

38. Ibid., 19–20.

39. Ibid., 18.

40. Ibid., 24–25

41. Ibid., 27–28.

42. Ibid., 29.

43. Jacques Lusseyran, *Against the Pollution of the I,* trans. Rob Baker (New York: Parabola Books, 1999), 40

44. Lusseyran, *And There Was Light*, 34. I apologize for leaving the construction as it is here. My insertion of a feminine pronoun for inclusivity would have made for extremely awkward reading.

45. Gerber, *Vibrational Medicine,* 52–53.

46. Ibid., 52–56.

47. Donald Nichol, *Holiness* (New York: Seabury Press, 1981), 22.

48. Ibid.

49. Ibid. See also a discussion of Gary Zukav's reflections on black holes in my book *In the Stillness You Will Know: Exploring the Paths of Our Ancient Belonging* (New York: Crossroad, 2002), 52–53.

50. Nichol, *Holiness,* 22.

51. Gail Bernice Holland, "The Rainbow Body," *IONS Noetic Science Review,* no. 59 (March–May 2002): 32.

52. They are referred to as "rainbow bodies" because of that.

53. Holland, "The Rainbow Body," 32; emphasis added.

54. IONS reports that "Francis Tisso holds the office of Canon in the Cathedral of St. Peter, Isernia, Italy, and is assigned to the archdiocese of San Francisco, where he is parochial vicar in Mill Valley."

55. Holland, "The Rainbow Body," 34.

56. Ibid.

57. Ibid. For a lengthy study in this regard also familiar to Tiso see Michael Murphy, *The Future of the Human Body: Exploration into the Further Evolution of Human Nature* (New York: Tarcher/Putman, 1992). Michael Murphy is co-founder of the Esalen Institute. His work is expansive and well documented.

58. David Steindl-Rast cited by Holland in "The Rainbow Body," 33.

59. Francis Tiso, "A Lecture on the Resurrection in Reference to the Rainbow Body Phenomenon," the Presidio Chapel, San Francisco, December 12, 2001, 2.

60. Ibid.

61. For more detailed discussion of matter as energy/light see Gerber, *Vibrational Medicine,* 56–67: "We are multidimensional beings. We are more than just flesh and bones, cells and proteins. We are beings in dynamic equilibrium with a universe of energy and light of many different frequencies and forms. We are composed of the stuff of the universe which, as we have already discovered, is actually 'frozen light.' Mystics throughout the ages have referred to us as beings of light. It is only now that science has begun to validate the basic premise behind this statement" (67).

62. Tiso, "A Lecture on the Resurrection," 5; emphasis added.

63. Teilhard de Chardin cited here by Willigis Jager, *Search for the Meaning of Life: Essays and Reflections on the Mystical*

Experience (Liguori, Mo.: Triumph Books, 1995), 24; emphasis added.

64. The vision was that of Canadian psychiatrist Richard Bucke cited here by Michael Murphy, *The Future of the Human Body,* 128–29. This account appeared in William James's 1902 lectures 16 and 17 (printed in *The Varieties of Religious Experience*) and was taken from a privately printed pamphlet that preceded Bucke's *Cosmic Consciousness,* where it appears in a slightly different form.

6. Walking into the Story

1. The origin of the story is unknown to me. It was shared with me during a conference by a participant who knew I would appreciate it.

2. Barbara Fiand, *Embraced by Compassion: On Human Longing and Divine Response* (New York: Crossroad, 1993), 128.

3. For those interested in the subject, good and lucid background reading can be found in any of the books by Bart D. Ehrman, especially *Lost Christianities: The Battle for Scripture and the Faiths We Never Knew* (New York: Oxford University Press, 2003); *The Orthodox Corruption of Scripture: The Effect of Early Christological Controversies on the Text of the New Testament* (New York: Oxford University Press, 1993). Books written in a simpler style are Marcus J. Borg's *The Heart of Christianity: Rediscovering a Life of Faith* (2003) and *Jesus, A New Vision: Spirit, Culture, and the Life of Discipleship* (1987), both from HarperSanFrancisco, as well as numerous others of a similar genre.

4. Ehrman, *Lost Christianities,* 217.

5. Ibid., 237.

6. Ibid., 1.

7. Borg, *Jesus, a New Vision,* 6.

8. Ibid., 7–8; emphasis added.

9. Werner Heisenberg showed that "depending upon how we look at it, a subatomic entity displays the properties of both a particle and a wave." It cannot be identified independently without taking the observer into consideration. Given this

discovery, physics moves away from the notion of objective observation and closer to a sense of participation where observer and observed mutually imply each other.

10. Walter Wink, *The Human Being: Jesus and the Enigma of the Son of the Man* (Minneapolis: Fortress Press, 2002), 7; emphasis added.

11. Ibid., 8.

12. I am using the term "projection" here in its psychological sense of "attributing one's own traits or attitudes to others." The power of projection is increased by its unconscious nature. I see either the good or the evil, which is in me but hidden from my awareness, in another and admire or reject him or her accordingly.

13. Wink, *The Human Being*, 11.

14. As well as of diverse scholarly interpretations of these perspectives researched and presented "in order to discern the past in its present meaning" (ibid., 8).

15. Barbara Fiand, *Prayer and the Quest for Healing: Our Personal Transformation and Cosmic Responsibility* (New York: Crossroad, 1999), 8.

16. Ibid.

17. Barbara Fiand, *In the Stillness You Will Know: Exploring the Paths of Our Ancient Belonging* (New York: Crossroad, 2002), 130.

18. Wink, *The Human Being*, 14.

19. Norman Perrin, *Rediscovering the Teaching of Jesus* (New York: Harper & Row, 1967), 104–5.

20. Ibid., 104.

21. Ibid., 107–8.

22. Ibid., 106, 161.

23. Fiand, *In the Stillness You Will Know*, 132.

24. For a more detailed reflection on the post-resurrection Jesus and his message of liberation see my book *Prayer and the Quest for Healing*, chapter 17.

25. Mary T. Malone, *Women and Christianity: From 1000 to the Reformation*, vol. 2 (Maryknoll, N.Y.: Orbis, 2001), 204.

26. Garry Wills, *Papal Sin: Structures of Deceit* (New York: Doubleday, 2000), 141.

27. Ibid., 143.

28. Ibid.

29. Rohr describes "liminal space" in this article as "that place where all transformation happens. . . . True communitas [church] comes from having walked through liminality together — and coming out the other side — forever different."

30. See Augustine, *Enchiridion* 13, 41, where he argues for the virgin birth of Jesus — hence his sinlessness since he was "conceived without any fleshly pleasure and so he also remained free from any kind of defilement by original sin."

Of Related Interest

Diarmuid O'Murchu
CATCHING UP WITH JESUS
A Gospel Story for Our Time

In this sequel to *Quantum Theology,* O'Murchu shows us Jesus in a wholly new and creative way. He explains Jesus as the heart of the creative web of the universe and then offers imaginative dialogues and poetry that invite us to experience the wonder of the Quantum Christ.

"I find this book brilliant, liberating, and, most of all, truthful. O'Murchu presents us with a Christ worthy of the real one, a Christ who can lure humanity and history forward into a salvation that really feels like salvation — for all the peoples and all of creation."
— Richard Rohr, author of *Adam's Return*

ISBN 0-8245-2298-2, paperback

crossroad

Of Related Interest

Michael Crosby
CAN RELIGIOUS LIFE
BE PROPHETIC?

First Place Winner, Catholic Press Awards!

"This is the brave work of a truly committed and deeply honest brother religious. This book about the prophetic dimension of religious life is itself prophetic. Its analysis of the characteristics of the prophetic tradition and its relationship to religious life is fresh, clear, and challenging. ...Best of all, it is both highly readable and honestly gripping. My recommendation: Every religious community in the country should study this book together before they even think of making another major decision.

— Joan Chittister, author of
The Rule of Benedict: Insights for the Ages

ISBN 0-8245-2270-2, paperback

crossroad

Of Related Interest

Joan Chittister
THE RULE OF BENEDICT
Insights for the Ages

The Benedictine way, the author contends, "is the spirituality of the twenty-first century because it deals with issues facing us now — stewardship, relationships, authority, community, balance, work, simplicity, prayer, and spiritual and psychological development."

ISBN 0-8245-2503-5, paperback

Check your local bookstore for availability.
To order directly from the publisher,
please call 1-800-707-0670 for Customer Service
or visit our Web site at *www.cpcbooks.com*.
For catalog orders,
please send your request to the address below.

THE CROSSROAD PUBLISHING COMPANY
16 Penn Plaza, Suite 1550
New York, NY 10001

All prices subject to change.

crossroad